VOICES FOR PEACE

VOICES FOR PEACE
An Anthology

Edited by Anna Kiernan

Scribner

First published in Great Britain by Scribner, 2001
An imprint of Simon & Schuster UK Ltd
A Viacom Company

Scribner and design are trademarks of Macmillan Library Reference USA,
Inc., used under license by Simon & Schuster, the publisher of this work.

1 3 5 7 9 10 8 6 4 2

Simon & Schuster UK Ltd
Africa House
64–78 Kingsway
London WC2B 6AH

www.simonsays.co.uk

Simon & Schuster Australia
Sydney

A CIP catalogue record for this book is available from the British Library

ISBN 0-7432-3066-3

Typeset by Palimpsest Book Production Limited,
Polmont, Stirlingshire
Printed and bound in Great Britain by
Omnia Books Limited, Glasgow

CONTENTS

Publisher's Note   vii

One
Caryl Churchill, 'Lessons We've Learnt'   3
Paul Foot, 'Address to Media Workers Against
  the War (MWAW)'   5
Dominique Lapierre, 'Redressing the Balance'   11
Courttia Newland, 'Ledbury Street'   15
William Dalrymple, 'Scribes of the New Racism'   23
Ronan Bennett, 'Talking About Emotions'   29
Mark Steel, 'The Perils of Selective Grief'   35
Martin Bell, 'The Case for Disenthralment'   39
Chris Bellamy, 'We're All in this Together Now'   47
Katharine Hamnett, 'Not in My Name'   55
Assad Hafeez, 'Diaries from the Front Line'   57
Ahdaf Soueif, 'Nile Blues'   61

Two
Matthew Parris, 'The Bigger They Come,
  The Harder They Fall'   77
Adrian Mitchell, 'William Blake Says:
  Every Thing that Lives is Holy' and
  'To Whom It May Concern'   83
Terence Conran, 'An Eye for an Eye'   87
Annie Lennox, 'Peace. What is That?'   89

George Monbiot, 'The Case for Collateral Repairs' 93
Terry Jones, 'The Grammar of the War on Terrorism' 99
Suheir Hammad, 'First Writing Since' 105
Rachel Billington, 'Where does the Bombing Stop?' 115
Joseph Olshan, 'First Betrayal' 121
Ben Okri, '11 September 2001: Firebirth' 125
Natasha Walter, 'The Invisible Women' 129
Stephen Jay Gould, 'A Time of Gifts' 139

Three
Edward W. Said, 'Collective Passion' 145
Terry Waite, 'War is Easy' 153
Karen Armstrong, 'The True, Peaceful Face of Islam' 159
James Mawdsley, 'The Right to Judge?' 163
Rahul Mahajan and Robert Jensen,
  'Hearts and Minds: Avoiding a New Cold War' 171
David Bellamy, 'Real Aid, Fair Trade
  and the Green Renaissance' 179
Ziauddin Sardar, 'The Jihad for Peace' 185
Anita Roddick, 'Society is Only as Strong
  as its Weakest Link' 195
Paul Marsden, 'Pandora's Box' 201
Geoffrey Robertson, 'Make Law, Not War' 213
Richard Harries, Bishop of Oxford,
  'The Presence of Justice' 221
Jason Elliot, 'The Devil's Complaint' 225
Martin Wright and Jonathon Porritt,
  'A River Runs Through It' 231

Contributor's Notes 241
Editor's Biography 257

Publisher's Note

The terrorist attacks of September 11 united the world in its condemnation of such breathtaking acts of malice. New Yorkers hugged strangers in the streets and the Big Apple, briefly, became a village. In the numbed aftermath of the bombing, a neighbourly peace emerged. But the rhetoric for war, for a 'crusade' against terrorism, was soon to the fore and the ramparts were drawn up again and the bombs fell.

The issues in this particular war are complex. And a growing number of people want them debated. The contributors to this anthology do not speak as one voice, but they have in common the desire to explore more humane, thoughtful and just ways of reacting to the atrocities of September 11. Some are experts in their fields of interest, such as Islam, international law, the Middle East or military studies, others have a strong connection with human rights organizations and still others represent the arts and humanities – playwrights, poets, actors, songwriters and novelists. Their viewpoints, backgrounds, creeds and beliefs are wonderfully disparate, a hymn to peace in itself, but also universally eloquent and passionate. We thank them so much for taking the time to contribute to

Voices for Peace. Thanks also go to War Child for their positive reception of the project and their helpfulness at every stage.

We hope that this anthology will help to engender the debate that democracy has so far denied us, and that it will lead to a discussion of the wider issues and cultural questions which frame this 'war against terrorism', issues which will not disappear with military victory on either side. All hope that this war will end quickly and with as little human suffering as possible, but should this come to pass, achieving a meaningful, lasting peace will entail a long, hard-fought battle that we can ill-afford to ignore.

Helen Gummer
Non Fiction Publisher
Simon & Schuster UK

If we could love even those who have attacked us, and seek to understand why they have done so, what then would be our response? Yet if we meet negativity with negativity, rage with rage, attack with attack, what then will be the outcome? These are the questions that are placed before the human race today. They are questions that we have failed to answer for thousands of years. Failure to answer them now could eliminate the need to answer them at all.

The Dalai Lama

One

Only thin smoke without flame
From the heaps of couch-grass;
Yet this will go onward the same
Through Dynasties pass.

Yonder a maid and her wight
Come whispering by:
War's annals will cloud into night
Ere their story die.

'In Time of
"The Breaking of Nations"',
Thomas Hardy

Lessons We've Learnt

If someone attacks your country, it's because of your country's good qualities not its bad ones.

When someone may have committed a crime, drop bombs on the country where he lives.

Extradition of a suspect to a third country is not acceptable if the evidence is not very good.

Better get him in your own country where you know he's guilty.

It is better to do something that makes things worse than to do nothing.

In a democracy, the leader decides whether to go to war.

Killing innocent people is an attack on civilization unless your side does it, then it's collateral damage.

The Pentagon and the twin towers were nothing to do with the military or capitalism.

Voices for Peace

Terrorism is killing by people without planes of their own.

Bombing and causing death by starvation win hearts and minds.

Strawberry jam and face wipes save millions from famine.

Countries that abuse human rights can be attacked if they don't have much support or sell us oil.

If there's a country you've been bombing for ten years, evidence is likely to emerge that it needs attacking some more.

New foreign policy that emerges after terrorism was always in place because terrorism can't achieve anything.

The risk of starvation for millions is less than the risk of hesitation for a leader.

Talking to the enemy is difficult; so is killing them, but it makes better television.

War is different from terrorism because war is bigger.

Caryl Churchill

Address to Media Workers
Against the War (MWAW)

One of the many disadvantages of the present situation is that we have to endure endless television footage of President Bush. Bush has a look on his face that is usually interpreted as a sign of distress at what happened on September 11. It is only after you've seen him again and again that you realize that the look does not represent distress at all. What it represents is panic: panic that he will not be able to summon up a word that even remotely approximates to the message he wishes to convey. So, for instance, in his first appearance after the atrocity in New York, he referred to the 'cowardly acts' of the terrorists. Someone might have taken him on one side and said well, you know, George, the people who hijacked the airliners are all dead by their own hand. You can call them lots of things, but you can't really call them cowards. So 'cowards' came down to 'folks', and then in one desperate moment 'evil doers'. This same uncertainty and vacillation seemed to paralyse the reaction to the bombings in New York so that for a moment it was possible to hope that there might, somewhere in the bowels of the United States government, be some grain of sanity.

All those hopes were a bit sad, really. Having an

imbecile for a president is a little embarrassing for the military-industrial complex that governs the US. So now we are at war, apparently to root out the horror of New York. I would define that horror as reckless bombing without warning which leads to the mass murder of innocent people. As a result, every night on the television there are the familiar pictures of explosions in the night air, superannuated generals discussing tactics, endless talk about precision bombing, targeting terrorists, humanitarian missions, international law. And already we can see what it all means: reckless bombing without warning which leads to the mass murder of innocent people.

There is another feature of war that is also familiar: the awful unanimity of people who call themselves our representatives. On Monday, the day the war broke out in Afghanistan, lots of speeches were made by MPs of all parties. Not a single voice was raised against the waging of war by Britain, the United States and other Western countries against one of the poorest countries on earth. Tony Blair can go on saying, until he strangles in his own rhetoric, that we are not waging war on the Afghan people, but all the brilliant brains among his advisers cannot explain how you drop bombs on Afghan cities without killing Afghan people. He can talk about humanitarian aid, but cannot explain how the dropping of food rations can feed 7 million starving people, many of them rushing desperately away from their homes to avoid the bombs.

Not a single voice was raised in Parliament against the declaration of war. On that unanimous afternoon last Monday, there was only one rude noise. It came from Paul Marsden, the Labour MP for Shrewsbury and Atcham. Mr Marsden, a mild enough man, asked on a point of order if perhaps there might be a vote. 'There is,' he said, 'growing disquiet that for the third time Parliament has been recalled, yet Honourable Members have been denied a vote on this war. Can you confirm to me that there will be no vote?' Here is the reply of Mr Speaker, guardian of the cradle of British democracy: 'It seems that the Honourable Gentleman is getting advice already. Procedural advice is best given privately at the chair. If the Honourable Gentleman wishes to come to the chair I will give him some private advice.' I heard that exchange on the radio; the Speaker's answer was greeted with howls of mirth from the Honourable Members, delighted that such an impertinent suggestion from a little-known backbencher should be so firmly put in its place. The result is that British forces have gone to a war in a far-off country for which there is little justification, and their and our representatives are not even allowed a vote on the matter.

This unanimity does not reflect what is going on in the country at large. The opposition to these attacks goes very deep, far deeper than any of the government ministers imagine. It is only a sign of the deep unease, doubt and, in some cases, fear that nags at the minds of ordinary people as they go to their daily jobs.

Some say: what is the alternative? The New York massacre was a terrible event and we are asked – well, what would you do? Would you appease the terrorists, leave the field open to them? Our reply is no, not at all. We can suggest to Bush, Blair and all the rest of them a whole series of policies that, we guarantee, would do immeasurably more to stop terrorists than bombing the countries in which they live. First, cut off your aid to the state of Israel and its merciless persecution of the Palestinian people. Stop grovelling to the war criminal Sharon. Stop shaking his blood-stained hand. Do all that is in your power to stop Mr Putin and his KGB in Russia from slaughtering and torturing the people of Chechnya. For that matter stop propping up dictatorships in Pakistan, Saudi Arabia and South Asia. Above all, instead of talking yet again about a new world order, set about dismantling economic and social priorities which divide the world, yes even our own world in Britain and in the United States, into classes: grossly rich minorities in power selling each other the weapons of mass destruction so that they can more ruthlessly control and punish the landless unarmed masses of the dispossessed. These are policies that hold out some hope of subverting terrorism. They are the exact opposite of the policies pursued by our governments. There is a most vital and urgent need to turn the hearts and minds of the British people against individual terrorism of the type that bombed New York and state terrorism of the type that is bombing Afghanistan.

Ten years ago, as the bombs started to rain down on Baghdad, John Pilger and I wrote a letter to the *Guardian* asking anyone who worked in the media and who shared our disgust at the war to come and talk to us in the Conway Hall. Five hundred people turned up that night and there and then we formed Media Workers Against the War. Our aims were simple: in general to oppose the war by every means at our disposal and in particular to do so in the media.

The situation today is far more intense than it was ten years ago. People are at once far more anxious and far more angry. Anti-war groups are forming all over the country. Media Workers Against the War will be part of a grand alliance of everyone against this war. It needs to be more effective, more powerful than before. We can and must challenge the government and force them, by the sheer weight of public pressure, to get their bombs and missiles out of Afghanistan and concentrate on economic and social policies that will lead to a world free from capitalist exploitation and free from racism, barbarism and terrorism.

Paul Foot

Redressing the Balance

It was in a slum in the Indian city of Bhopal, among the survivors of history's greatest industrial disaster, that I saw the horrifying images of September 11. I witnessed live coverage of the dreadful terrorist attacks on New York and Washington on television in the company of men and women who had undergone a similar apocalypse eighteen years previously. Their crisis resulted from a gas leak from an American pesticide plant built almost in the heart of their city that killed between 16,000 and 30,000 people.

Of course, the tragedy bore no resemblance to the appalling attack by Osama bin Laden's men. The American engineers who had deactivated all the safety systems of their hi-tech Indian plant in order to cut costs had no intention of killing anyone. Nevertheless their foolish negligence caused five or six times as many deaths as the terrorist attacks in New York and Washington.

But who remembers Bhopal? Who ever led a world-wide crusade to bring those who were responsible for that crime – and it was a crime – before a court, so that their victims might at least know how and why their disaster came about? Warren Anderson, the

President of Union Carbide at the time of the catastrophe, fled from his Florida retreat when Interpol issued a warrant for his arrest. The authorities concerned are not interested in knowing where he is hiding and the Bhopal victims have no hope of ever obtaining his extradition. What is more, no international body is backing their efforts. There is nothing very unusual about that. After all, what is an Indian life worth? The *Wall Street Journal* tried to work it out once: 'Given that an American life is worth approximately 500,000 dollars and that India's GNP is only 1.7% of that of the United States, it may be estimated that an Indian life is only worth 8,000 dollars.'

The Bhopal martyrs never had the opportunity to prick the conscience of the universe. They were the victims of what is coyly referred to as an 'industrial accident', whereas the World Trade Center martyrs are those of a deliberate act of terrorism. Above all, though, the Bhopal martyrs had the misfortune of being predominantly poor. And it is a well-known fact that the voices of the poor do not carry much weight in this world, when a billion men, women and children do not have access to drinking water; a quarter of the inhabitants have less than one dollar a day to survive on and where one child in a rich country consumes as much as fifty times more than a child in the Third World.

It was despicable religious fanaticism that armed the New York and Washington assassins. But from where did these fanatics draw their resolve, if not from the poverty and injustice that afflicts a broad area of our planet? I would not want to be in Calcutta on the day when a figure with the charisma of Gandhi, but the violence of Osama bin Laden, rallies the slum-dweller to revolt. On that day the Park Street shop windows, brimful of luxury goods, and the villas in the smart neighbourhoods will be pillaged and their owners massacred in an explosion of rage, that has been stifled for too long. The revolt of the poor of Calcutta might then spread throughout India and the world, extending everywhere that downtrodden, despised and humiliated people decide that they have had enough of their inhumane living conditions.

To understand the causes of the violence that brings daily bloodshed to the land where prophets and Christ himself preached love and reconciliation we must look to the lives led by Palestinian refugees who are squatting in sordid ghettos. Look to Mother Teresa's soup kitchens in the poorest areas of London, New York, Paris, Rome or Rio de Janeiro to assess the state of extreme despair in which a substantial proportion of humanity finds itself.

In New York's Bronx district, less than an hour's journey from the twin towers, I was shocked to encounter misery, poverty and a wretchedness beyond mere financial deprivation. When people find themselves cut off from all humane reference points, bereft of identity, religion, nationality, family, past and future, they become pariahs. Should we really be surprised when fanatics, under the guise of perverted religious ideals, have no reservations about tying sticks of dynamite to their waists in the middle of innocent crowds or hijacking passenger planes to launch them at targets which represent the values they abhor?

The problems of poverty and injustice in two-thirds of our planet remain unresolved. At the beginning of this millennium, the greatest and primary challenge confronting the West is how to share its abundance with less fortunate countries. Procedures must be established to ensure that the proceeds reach those for whom they are really intended. The question remains: can we act before it is too late? For only when the millions of underprivileged in the world have won their right to dignity and happiness may we glimpse the dawn of true peace between peoples.

Dominique Lapierre

Ledbury Street

I wrote this story for the Artthrob: Defining a Nation tour, but feel that the events it depicts are relevant to the current situation concerning Muslims in this country. Although Britain is very much a multicultural society in terms of diversity, tolerance of varied cultures has never been anywhere near total, even in the most ethnically strong areas. The recent riots in Oldham and the Brixton nail bombing attack are testimony to that fact. My story is an appeal for tolerance from all sides, and a hope that, as individuals, we begin to see all people in the same way instead of making assumptions based on perceived class, creed, racial and sexual generalizations. If we can't get over that most basic and fundamental of human urges – to make someone else the enemy – then maybe we are doomed indeed.

*   *   *

I remember Ledbury Street like every day was yesterday, and the years were simply hours, the decades morning, afternoon, night. I grew from a child to become a teenager and eventually a man on that row of council houses, a suburban road in the midst of urban decay. Ledbury Street was a Garden of Eden, slap-bang in the middle of the sprawling concrete jungle that was London. A quiet cul-de-sac, where us kids were in training for the world that we'd one day inhabit as full-grown adults. The community around us was rich and varied; this, like everything else on my road was broken down and duplicated, so we became miniature doppelgängers of the society surrounding us.

Recently, a local reporter came down and interviewed Ledbury Street's residents. He was writing a piece on the changing face of Britain and felt our street was a microcosm of multicultural society. I had lived there so long I remained loyal to the image we strove to maintain and didn't challenge him on his view. If he really knew what Ledbury Street was like, I'm sure his story would have radically changed, and changed for the worse. I often wondered if he would have reported what he found. For life in Ledbury Street was not as it seemed.

My parents moved on to the street sometime in the early 70s. They had worked for years, buying our house on a modest mortgage. I was three years old at the time. My brothers were six and nine. I never found out if the three-year gaps were fate, or one of mum and dad's elaborate 'plans'. They were teenage sweethearts, whose affection had never waned, and they'd come to England in the 60s full of expectation. Despite the hardships of the ice-cold climate, they found somewhere to live, jobs and friends. My home was a happy one, my upbringing influenced by hard work.

The difference in our ages was sufficient to make my brothers and myself semi-strangers for most of our lives. We had varying tastes in music, clothes and friends. I never felt left out, for I had my own little gang of childhood buddies, all of us closer than the fingers on one hand. The local council used our road as a testing ground for race relations; I swear there were families from almost every country on earth. It was made up of Irish, Italian, Spanish, Moroccan, English, West Indian, Pakistani, African, Chinese. It's true to say that to us kids, these differences didn't mean a thing, though by the time we were old enough for primary school, we did notice. Over the years, they enhanced our friendships. I learnt to say *Bacra di culo* and *Hacclada Nebe* . . . which means kiss my arse in Italian, fuck off in Moroccan. My education was sweeter than nectar, and just as plentiful. I wallowed in a sea of cultures and language.

Of course, out of all those kids, there were a few closer to me than the others. Some of them became friends that I still possess today. Fate had thrown us together, so we discovered life at the same time, but from separate angles that were reinforced by the teachings of our families. I'm sure my thirst for travel was preceded by my experiences, whetting my appetite like my first sip of lager, aged nine.

There was Danny Rosenfield, the cockney kid that lived next door, with his twin sister, older brother and taxi-driver dad. His mother was a dinner lady at the local secondary school. Some evenings she'd send Danny's twin, Charlotte, to our house with left-over pudding, which made her a firm favourite with us boys. The Rosenfields were your typical East End characters – loud and chirpy, more like Barbara Windsor than

Dirty Den. Already on Ledbury when we arrived, my parents always reminded me that Danny's family came over on our first day, welcoming us to the street.

There were three Asian families on our road, but only one with a kid my age; Kabil, a crazy, perform-any-dare type of guy, who I loved to bits. He was a natural artist at heart, drawing portraits, caricatures and still-life pictures with a breathtaking talent that astounded everyone who saw them. His family was made up of three older brothers, two younger sisters. His father was a schoolteacher, his mother a house-wife, and they got on with everyone.

These boys were my closest friends. We made sure we went to the same secondary school, though we couldn't quite manage the same classes. I was split from the others and so made friends with a Black kid called Arron who lived on the estate behind Ledbury. Within no time, he was a regular visitor to our road. He made friends with Kabil and Danny and hung out with us as if Ledbury Street was his second home.

I must have been around fourteen that hot summer when everything changed. We were enjoying our six-week school holiday. I'd called for Arron early and we were walking towards Danny's house, talking loud, eager to play football and smoke weed in the nearby park. When we got to his front gate, we saw Danny's twin Charlotte sitting with her friends, a group of Black girls, on a multitude of deck-chairs. They were all dressed in summer clothing, shorts and T-shirts. The girls jumped to attention, but it wasn't for my benefit.

I forgot to tell you about Arron. The girls were mad

for him. He was the colour of manila, with an even white smile, curly black hair and large Bambi-brown eyes. He had long, curling eyelashes that really belonged on a girl. Girls wrote their initials on walls beside his, but Arron wasn't watching any of them. There was only one girl he liked – Charlotte, my best friend's sister.

Like a dark storm cloud brewing in the sky, the results of that day were inevitable. Arron sat beside Charlotte, making her blush, his intention plain. None of the girls was interested in me, so I went inside to talk to my mate. When we came out to the garden, the Black girls were still there, but Charlotte and Arron were gone.

The effects were almost immediate. Danny's reaction was one of deep anger, which I couldn't really work out. I mean, his sister had dated guys before – there were even some who claimed to have slept with her – and Danny had never gone mad, not once. Charlotte was her own person and the 'big brother' act didn't wash with her, especially since she was the eldest by two minutes. Danny insisted we look for the couple; we did, but never found them. Sometime that evening they came back hand-in-hand, treating each other with gentle affection. I found myself noticing the abrupt difference between their entwined brown and white fingers. I saw the anger on Danny's face and suddenly realized why.

The Rosenfields, as one, rallied against the relationship. Arron wasn't allowed in the house. Danny's older brother would bully him at school and on the streets; I caught him at it on many occasions. Of course, this reaction split the street into two very definite camps – those that agreed with the Rosenfields and those who did not. Charlotte and Arron refused to be cowed by this display of open racism and continued to see each other in secret, despite her parents. I grew closer to Charlotte as time went by; she was scared by her family's reaction, especially her father's. She realized they'd always harboured views she'd been unaware of.

This appalled my family. My father changed his tune, swearing that I was to stay away from Danny as long as Arron wasn't good enough for his sister. There became something of a feud, complete with snide glances, veiled threats and even a pushing and shoving match one time. Luckily, violence never erupted, but it was a close thing. Then something worse happened. Charlotte fell pregnant.

There was uproar for three months. Charlotte was ordered to stay in the house, with Arron visiting again and again, to be turned away each time. He'd come by my house and break down in tears in front of my trembling mother, saying he only wanted to do right by his son (he kept insisting the child was a boy). Then one day, Charlotte emerged from the house as if everything was back to normal. The gossip spread at once; she'd had an abortion, a miscarriage, a phantom pregnancy . . . One thing everyone was sure she *didn't* have was a baby. She went back to school in time for her mocks and passed.

This was a major blow to the sensitive racial balance on Ledbury Street. Families withdrew into their own homes; Black and White kids simply refused to mix. Charlotte was ostracized by her Black friends for at least a year, then they forgave her and accepted her as an honorary rudegyal. Charlotte left Ledbury Street not long after her exams. I heard she married an African and emigrated. As for my friendship with Danny and Kabil, it was never the same again. Kabil, in the same class as Danny, had sided with him throughout. This was something that amazed me and I didn't recover. We said hello when we saw each other, but we never hung out. I found a new set of friends through Arron, and they were all Black. Arron sunk into a depression from which I thought he'd never recover; he left school and got into the Nation, but left after six months. Last time I saw him, he was living in Finsbury Park with some Jewish girl. They wanted kids, but said they'd have them when they left the United Kingdom for good.

Courttia Newland

Scribes of the New Racism

September 25, 2001: Seidnaya is a Greek Orthodox convent in Syria, three hours' walk from Damascus. The monastery sits on a great crag of rock overlooking the orchards and olive groves of the Damascene plain, more like a Crusader castle than a place of worship.

According to legend, the monastery was founded in the sixth century after the Byzantine Emperor Justinian chased a stag on to the top of the hill during a hunting expedition. Just as Justinian was about to draw his bow, the stag changed into the Virgin Mary, who commanded him to build a convent on the rock. The abbey quickly become a place of pilgrimage. To this day streams of Christian, Muslim and Druze pilgrims trudge their way to Seidnaya from the mountains of Lebanon and the valleys of the Syrian jebel. A couple of years ago, while on a six-month tramp around the Middle East, I went to spend a night within its walls.

By the time I arrived at the abbey church, it was after eight o'clock on a dark and cold winter night. Two nuns in black veils were chanting from a lectern, while a priest, hidden behind the iconostasis, echoed their chants in a deep, reverberating bass. The only light came from a few flickering lamps suspended on gold chains.

Inside the church I witnessed a small miracle. The congregation in the church consisted not principally of Christians but almost entirely of heavily bearded Muslim men and their shrouded wives. As the priest circled the altar with his thurible, filling the sanctuary with great clouds of incense, the men bobbed up and down on their prayer mats as if in the middle of Friday prayers in a great mosque. Their women mouthed prayers from the shadows. Closely watching the Christian women, a few went up to the icons hanging from the pillars; they kissed them, then lit a candle and placed it in front of the image.

At the end of the service I saw a Muslim couple approach one of the nuns. The woman was veiled; only her nose and mouth were visible through the black wraps. Her husband, a burly man who wore his straggly beard without a moustache, looked remarkably like the wilder sort of Hezbollah commander featured in news bulletins from southern Lebanon. But whatever his politics, he carried in one hand a heavy tin of olive oil and in the other a large plastic basin full of fresh bread loaves, and he gave both to the nun as an offering, bowing his head as shyly as a schoolboy and retreating backwards in blushing embarrassment.

It was an extraordinary sight, yet this was, of course, the old way. The Eastern Christians, the Jews and the Muslims have lived side by side in the Levant for nearly one and a half millennia and have only been able to do so because of a degree of mutual tolerance and shared customs unimaginable in the solidly Christian West. The same broad tolerance that had given homes to the hundreds of thousands of penniless Jews expelled by the bigoted Catholic kings of Spain and Portugal protected the Eastern Christians in their ancient homelands despite the Crusades and the almost continual hostility of the Christian West.

Every schoolchild knows that the closest medieval Europe ever came to a multicultural or multi-religious society was Islamic Spain and Sicily; but it is perhaps less well known that, as late as the eighteenth century, European visitors to the Mogul and Ottoman Empires were astounded by the degree of religious tolerance that they found there. As Monsieur de la Motraye, a Huguenot exile escaping religious persecution in Europe, put it: 'There is no country on earth where the exercise of all religions is more free and less subject to being troubled than in Turkey.' If that coexistence was not always harmonious, it was at least a kind of pluralist equilibrium that simply has no parallel in European history.

I have been thinking of Seidnaya a lot since the atrocity at the World Trade Center. Since then we have seen virulent Islamophobia, as a hundred 'experts' in Islam have popped up to offer their views on a religion few seem ever to have encountered in person. A whole series of leaders and comment pieces have denounced Islam, while always being careful to state that the fundamentalists and terrorists do not, of course, represent the views of 'decent Muslims'.

Prejudices against Muslims and the spread of idiotic

stereotypes of Muslim behaviour and beliefs have been developing at a frightening rate in the last decade, something the horrific assault on the World Trade Center can only exacerbate. Anti-Muslim racism now seems in many ways to be replacing anti-Semitism as the principal Western expression of bigotry against 'the Other'.

The horrific massacre of 8,000 Muslims, some unarmed, at Srebrenica in 1995, never led to a stream of pieces about the violence and repressive tendencies of Christianity. Equally the extraordinary size and diversity of the Islamic world should caution against lazy notions of a united, aggressive Islam acting in concert against 'the Judaeo-Christian West'.

Islam is no more cohesive than Christendom: neither is it a single, rational, antagonistic force. We are different from the Swedes, the Serbs and the fundamentalist evangelicals of the American Midwest; so the Indonesians are totally different from the Mauritanians and the Hezbollah headbangers of Lebanon. There is no such thing as 'the Muslim mind', anti-democratic, terrorist, primeval in its behaviour, or however else it is portrayed, versus a rational, peace-loving 'Christian mind'. The Islamic world, for better or worse, is much like anywhere else in the developing world.

For 1400 years there has been a debate within Islam between liberal and orthodox approaches. What is clear, in recent years, is that insensitive and clumsy Western interference in the Islamic world almost always strengthens the hands of the fundamentalists and the conservatives against those who represent more liberal and enlightened interpretations of Islam.

Already we are seeing Pakistan being pushed to the verge of a fundamentalist Islamic revolution as its military government is bullied into helping the Americans against their Afghan kinsmen. Insensitive rhetoric of the kind we have seen in the press, and the use by President Bush of the word 'crusade', can only strengthen the hands of the fundamentalists, fatally weakening the secular states of the region. Most Muslim states would support a precise surgical assault on Osama bin Laden's al-Qaeda network; they would not put up with a large-scale ground war in Afghanistan or Iraq. We must proceed with the greatest of caution. Such a war is much more likely to destabilize the entire region than to achieve the intended aims.

William Dalrymple

Talking About Emotions

As I write this, Tony Blair's speech to the Welsh Assembly is being broadcast live on radio. Concerned that British support for the US-led air strikes against Afghanistan is waning, the Prime Minister is attempting to stiffen the nation's moral fibre and get people 'to stay the course'. 'It is important,' he is saying, 'that we never forget why we have done this, never forget how we felt as we watched planes fly into the trade towers, never forget those answerphone messages, never forget how we imagined how mothers told their children they were going to die.' The intention is clearly to invite a gut-level response and comes close to encouraging revenge.

At the same time as Blair was putting the finishing touches to his speech, a reporter in Kabul was filing a story on the latest US air strikes. It is worth quoting the piece at length, partly because it plainly contradicts US Defense Secretary Donald Rumsfeld's claim that the Taliban are manipulating journalists by getting women to sit by bomb sites and shed tears of manufactured grief; partly because, unusually in the reporting of the war so far, it acknowledges that 'their' dead had loves and histories, just like 'ours'; but also because it is a perfect illustration that the other side too have emotions.

American air strikes meant to punish the Taliban spilled over today into residential neighbourhoods here, killing thirteen civilians. It was the second time in two days that missiles have hit homes and killed residents . . . Weeping families buried their dead within hours of the morning bombardment . . . 'I have lost all my family,' said a sobbing woman in the Qalaye Khatir neighbourhood on Kabul's northern edge. 'I am finished.' After the morning strikes, a father hugged the dead body of his son, who looked barely two. Women slapped themselves with grief. One 13-year-old boy, Jawad, bandaged and bloody from the strike, asked about his relatives – not knowing he was the only survivor in his nine-member family. Jawad lay semiconscious in his bed in Wazir Akbar Khan hospital in Kabul. A neighbour, Muhammad Razi, explained to a journalist that Jawad was unaware of all that had happened. 'He asked me, "How is my family?"' Mr Razi whispered. 'I said: "They are all OK. You were walking in your sleep, and you fell down the well by your house, and I rescued you."' . . . In Washington, Pentagon spokesmen had no immediate comment on the latest strikes and the civilian casualties involved. The Pentagon has stressed that civilians are never deliberately targeted.

It is possible that Mr Razi will come to the semi-conscious Jawad's hospital bedside to bring him the comforting news that he wasn't deliberately targeted. Who knows, it may even be possible that Mr Razi will tell Jawad of Blair's speech today, from which Jawad will learn that the West is 'morally right' and, if he only makes the effort to understand, he will accept the reasons for the unfortunate obliteration of his family.

It is, however, as we all know, much more likely that Jawad – if his hospital is not bombed and he has the good fortune to survive a conflict we are now being told may last for our lifetimes – will also 'never forget'. He will never forget that he once had a home, that he once had parents and brothers and sisters. And like the father cradling his 2-year-old son, like the 'finished' woman who lost all her family, he will never forget that an American bomb blasted those he loved to bits and a British Prime Minister went on radio to emote about morality and right and justice.

If Jawad rejects the Pentagon's bland avowals and Blair's words as hypocrisy and cant, if he grows up with a visceral hatred of America and Britain and the West, who will blame him? Who in the West would dare say to him, 'I know we killed your family, Jawad, but Britain is your friend. America is your friend'? The dead cannot bear grudges, but those who loved them can, and do. That's what tends to happen when you bomb people.

We are being urged never to forget. Emotions are being deliberately heated. Is this really the way to go? The Irish experience strongly suggests it is not. The high emotions sparked by deaths on 'our' side resulted directly in deaths on 'theirs'. 'We' struck back. 'They' struck back again, only harder this time. Before we knew it we were in what the rest of the world was telling us was a 'self-perpetuating cycle of violence'. British politicians whose emotions were not quite at the same pitch condemned 'tit-for-tat' killings and wondered why the two communities could not forgive, forget and, like decent, civilized people in the rest of the decent, civilized world, move on.

There were many reasons why they could not – injustice and discrimination, being among the most important. But just as important was the emotion which sustained and fuelled the conflict. Emotion, as the Prime Minister's advisers, if they are doing their jobs properly, should very quickly point out to him, works on both sides, 'ours' and 'theirs'. When what we feel becomes what is true and what is true becomes what is right, barbarism and savagery are validated. Emotion blots out understanding, analysis, good sense. It makes a thousand times more difficult the serious business of resolving conflicts and ending enmities and hatreds. Emotional responses cannot be turned on and off when political practicalities and military exigencies demand reversals in policy. We are accustomed to talking about 'taking the heat out of a situation' in order to find political settlements. Emotion does the opposite of this.

Do we never forget the dead? Is it right that the dead must always be remembered? In Ireland, the memory of the executed rebel leaders of the 1916 Rising helped create and sustain the Anglo-Irish war of independence, in which yet more volunteers fell. They in turn were remembered (indeed, very recently ten of the Irish fallen were remembered in a state ceremony, which attracted much hostility from anti-Republican commentators). In the Troubles there are so many to remember. Just look in the In Memoriam columns of the newspapers.

I can remember one of the dead very clearly, though he was no more than an acquaintance. I said good evening to him as I was on my way to the pictures with my girlfriend. This was March 1974. On the bus on the way back, we heard a thunderous blast. I jumped off and ran towards the sound of the explosion. Dazed people, covered in dust, a few crying but most merely numb (the grey men and women making their way north after the attacks on the World Trade Center were eerily familiar to me). A Loyalist gang had rolled a beer keg filled with explosive into Conway's bar on the Shore Road, near where I lived. The dead man had calmly and bravely picked it up and taken it outside. The bomb went off in his arms and he was, literally, blown to pieces. The next morning firemen scraped sticky bits of what looked like burned rubber from the walls of the bar and shops. They scraped and dug this man's blasted, charred flesh in the way you do when you are stripping wallpaper, and with as much ceremony. They had seen it all before. But among those who knew the dead man was there an emotional response? Of course there was. I heard what people were saying. I felt in my own bones horror and anger. I don't know if there was a death on 'their' side directly attributable to this death on 'ours', but at the very least it kept alive the fears and hatreds on which the conflict thrived.

It has taken more than a generation for the emotions provoked by deaths like this to subside to the point where negotiation and the pursuit of peaceful methods has all but replaced retaliation and revenge. The heat is slowly being taken out of the equation. Blair has played his part in this. And the dead? They are not yet forgotten, and perhaps they never will be. But at least their deaths are no longer being used – emotionally, as some would say; cynically as others might – to legitimize the infliction of yet more deaths.

Tony Blair has made high moral purpose and emotion his rhetorical trademark. Until now when it has missed its target – as at the Women's Institute fiasco – the collateral damage has been minimal and the main casualty has been the Prime Minister himself. But this is different. Lives are at stake, 'ours' and 'theirs'.

Ronan Bennett

The Perils of Selective Grief

Dare to suggest that there may just possibly be a slight link between America's past behaviour and the hijackings, and out pour the accusations. Such people are guilty of 'foaming malevolence' according to one paper. Because all decent reporters know the only humanitarian response is to shake your head, mutter a sentence containing the words 'evil' and 'monsters' and demand that someone somewhere gets bombed.

Maybe they argue amongst themselves, these types. Perhaps they approach a fellow columnist and say 'How callous to describe the terrorists as "evil" when they're at least "despicably evil": though I care more than anyone because I wrote "words can't describe this despicable evil". Top that.'

Strangely, many of those who appear the most horrified haven't always been so sensitive about the loss of innocent lives. They managed to watch the Gulf War on telly, for example, and even seemed to enjoy the experience. I wonder whether Iraqi TV showed the New York disaster in the same way we covered the bombing of Baghdad. Maybe a panel of experts sat around a table chatting about the extraordinary accuracy of the pilots, while the presenter said 'And we're being told that so far there's not a single Iraqi casualty, so that really is fantastic news isn't it?'

Some people are almost poetic in their selective grief. On Radio 4 one morning we were treated to an 'adviser' to Vladimir Putin, sombrely running through his evils and despicables, beside himself with bewilderment at how anyone could cause such carnage. Well, if I was his counsellor I might suggest he work through his confusion by asking the bloke he advises, who slaughtered 50,000 civilians in the town of Grozny. Not that I'm calling him a hypocrite as maybe he only advises Putin on traffic-flow issues, but it does make you wonder who's going to pop up next. 'With us in the studio is Harold Shipman, who's issued his own statement condemning the terrorists' "appalling disregard for human life". Harold, thank you for joining us on this awful, awful occasion.'

Some Palestinians were so malicious they danced in the streets, raged the newspaper that screamed 'Gotcha!' following the drowning of 300 conscripted Argentinians. It could be argued that was different, as they weren't civilians. But the 500 women and children blasted by a cruise missile in a Baghdad bomb shelter certainly were. As were countless Nicaraguans, or the million Vietnamese, such as the victims in this account of the My Lai massacre: 'The killings began without warning. Soldiers began shooting women and children who were kneeling, weeping and praying round a temple. Villagers were killed in their homes. Helicopters shot down those who fled. Many of the GIs were laughing, "Hey, I got me another one. Chalk one up for me".

Soldiers took breaks to rest and smoke before resuming the killing.'

Maybe this was a long time ago and therefore irrelevant to today's story, except that when George Bush Sr launched the war against Iraq, he promised this 'won't be like Vietnam, where we were fighting with one hand tied behind our back'. And this has summed up their attitude ever since: 'we lost in Vietnam because we were too bloody liberal'. All that stopping for fags between killings, it's no wonder they lost.

Then there was Chile and Lebanon and so on; thousands of innocent people with innocent families, amongst them firemen and fathers and people with faces who were never displayed on the centre pages of the *Daily Mail*, never to be remembered during minute silences at the start of football matches.

So how can it be explained, this erratic caring of Presidents and advisers and those who are opposed to foaming malevolence? Could it be that their grieving is, perchance, in some way politically motivated? That they weep not for the devastated families, shell-shocked citizens and unimaginable torment of the victims, but in horror and disbelief that this could happen in America?

Now the selective grievers demand retribution, and don't seem too bothered whom it is against. The implication is that anything less than devastation of somewhere or other would be showing a lack of respect for the victims. Like manipulative teenage lovers, they're pleading 'Go on, you'd do it if you *really* cared.'

So, it looks as if Afghanistan will do for a start.

Though I can't see the point in bombing buildings there as the Taliban seem happy to blow them up themselves. After a cruise-missile strike, they'd probably send Bush a note saying 'Cheers George, that saved us doing that infidel street, with its provocative curvy bit.'

So now atrocity is likely to be answered with atrocity, together with all the inevitable webs of lies bound up as part of a package. Already we're told the CIA satellites can 'pinpoint a cigarette'. Really? Yet they haven't the foggiest idea where Osama bin Laden is. I suppose the one thing they didn't reckon on was that he doesn't smoke. If only he stopped for one occasionally between killings they'd have him in a flash.

We can be, and as humans should be, extraordinarily moved by all the victims. But if we're only extraordinarily moved by the victims on one side, we're at least halfway to foaming.

Mark Steel

The Case for Disenthralment

I wish to raise a dissenting if broadly peace-minded voice. Those who destroyed the World Trade Center and killed so many thousands are not, in my view, open to mediation and negotiation. If they find another target of opportunity they will strike at it just as ruthlessly. That target is more likely to be civilian than military. There will be further casualties. Here we are in a new world, a world of asymmetric warfare in which the traditional brokering of ceasefires and compromises simply does not apply. The United Nations has been sidelined, not just by the decision of the principal target and the last remaining superpower, but also by the revolutionary nature of the conflict itself.

The events of September 11 represented the most devastating attack on the continental United States by an outside power since the British burned the White House in 1812. With the exception of the Civil War the Americans have waged their wars abroad, often at sacrificial cost, but the homeland was untouched. It was also scarcely conceivable, because of the dynamics of democracy, that force would not be met with force. President Jimmy Carter was denied a second term because of perceived weakness in dealing with the hostage crisis in Tehran in 1980. This time the bombs were bound to fall, and they did.

I do not doubt that in this case the use of force against force is justified, if only to take the initiative from those who seek to destroy us. The option of inaction is not available. It is a principle of warfare that, if you wait for bad things to happen, bad things will happen. Any government's primary duty is to protect its people, whether from threats new or old. If it fails in that it will fall. Another principle of warfare is that a military operation, if it is to succeed, needs an achievable objective. To take two examples from World War II: the Dieppe raid did not have an achievable objective; the Normandy landings did. The question in this case is: what is the achievable objective of the American bombing campaign, other than to satisfy a need to avenge the deaths of New York's firefighters – and to rally support for the enemy when the bombs go astray? From my personal experience of warfare, I am as unconvinced about the bombing strategy as about the deployment of ground troops, other than small groups of special forces as advisers to anti-Taliban units or on limited and specific missions informed by good intelligence.

I doubt very much whether a ground campaign, fighting from cave to cave, is operationally possible. Military commanders try to avoid street fighting, because of the cost in lives. Cave fighting against the soldiers of the jihad, except on limited operations and with accurate intelligence, seems equally questionable. A further inhibition belongs to the nature of asymmetric warfare.

The two sides are not in fact evenly matched in their military cultures. Casualties matter so much more to one than to the other.

This is not Hollywood. There is no Rambo or Terminator to save the day for the Americans after the last commercial break. This is the real world. And in the real world there is an imbalance of forces, with the firepower favouring one side and the fanaticism another. If we seek to wage a conventional war we may not even win in conventional terms. We should know that and understand it.

It would be wiser, in my view, to think of this thing differently, and to go back for a paradigm to the American Civil War. At the height of that terrible conflict the American president made a speech which Aaron Copland included in the narration for his 'Portrait of Abraham Lincoln', and which speaks to our present predicament as eloquently as anything I have come across. Lincoln said: 'As our case is new, we must think anew and act anew. We must disenthrall ourselves.'

We, too, could use some disenthralment from the view that armed conflict has to end with the victory of one side over another, or with a peace agreement, or with both. This one may not. I expect this campaign, which is as much a clash of ideas as of arms, to endure in one form or another for the rest of my life – and I am not planning to meet my Maker imminently. It will certainly not satisfy the clamour of the media, in an age of rolling news and ratcheting expectations, for quick results and a Kosovo-style conclusion. It may possibly happen that extraordinary luck and intelligence will deliver up Osama bin Laden, dead or alive – but if dead, others will take the martyr's place; if alive, the conflict will continue and no international criminal court yet exists before which he could be brought. (The Americans themselves opposed its establishment.)

We could use some further disenthralment from the idea that technology conquers all, and that wars can be waged without costs and casualties – on our own side, that is. It is worth remembering that the attack on the World Trade Center was not the only case of mass murder in recent years. Rather more people, about 7000, were killed in the Srebrenica massacre of 1995. Yet we responded to one with bombs and missiles, aircraft carriers and commando raids – and to the other with a shrug of the shoulders. We walked away from a UN-declared safe area, in a country that had more than 30,000 UN troops in it. It was as if we were saying, British and French and Dutch lives matter on one scale of values, and Bosnian lives on another. So today, New York is worth going to war for, and if as many innocent lives are lost in Afghanistan that's just collateral damage. We stand for certain values in the Western democracies, or at least we claim to, and if in defending those values we sacrifice them, then we revert to the notorious Vietnam example of saving a village by destroying it. George Orwell is worth rereading in this context. In his marvellous essay on 'Politics and the English Language' the euphemism was 'pacification'. Today it's 'collateral damage'.

In the matter of disenthralment, we should also disenthral ourselves from the notion that we in the Western
democracies enjoy peace and freedom as a God-given
right. Of course we don't. Peace and freedom, as we
understand them, are not a right but a privilege. They
have to be fought for; politically if we can, but militarily if we cannot, and certainly not taken for granted.
If we take them for granted we shall surely lose them.
Perhaps we have just grown soft and complacent. We
have such a stronger sense of our rights than we do of
our obligations. My own view, from where I have been
and what I have seen since the end of the Cold War,
is that the new world order is immeasurably more
dangerous than the old. We have been living in a fool's
paradise or golden age – perhaps the same thing seen
from a different angle. There is not one of us whose
life is not touched and changed by the present emergency. It is a wake-up call to us all. For that reason
alone we have to hope that some good will come of it.

I should make it clear that I am not writing here for
UNICEF, whom I am proud to serve as an occasional
envoy and witness. But six weeks after the disasters in
New York and Washington, it was a journey for
UNICEF that brought home to me the gravity and
novelty of the challenge we face. It is time to throw
the rulebooks away. Neither Clausewitz nor manuals
of peacekeeping have anything to teach us.

The frontier chosen by UNICEF was a place where
it was (and still is) active, together with the British
medical charity MERLIN. It was a flood plain of the
Pyandzh River between Afghanistan and Tadjikistan,

where at least 10,000 refugees were seeking shelter, with more arriving daily. It was a no man's land in a double sense. The Afghans had fled from a Taliban-held area, and had nowhere else to go. On a 300 foot escarpment above them the border was sealed not by Tadjik but by Russian troops. In the sense of realpolitik, it was Russia's southern frontier, closed to refugees, closed to Islamic fundamentalists, and to just about everyone except (occasionally) the volunteers from these two charities carrying out a programme of immunization. The flood plain was also a no man's land in that it had previously been thought uninhabitable. Now the Afghans were digging in for the winter, living in holes in the ground covered with river grasses, building mud huts against the winter weather. Water was scarce except from the river itself, under Taliban gunfire. There was little food but bread and oil, and not much of that. The sinister symptoms of scurvy were showing themselves.

I drove back north through part of Tadjikistan that used to be a desert. After two years of drought and the collapse of its Soviet irrigation system, it was returning whence it came, as much of a desert as large parts of Uzbekistan, Pakistan and Afghanistan itself. Misery and warfare march in the same legion. We ignore them at our peril. The time is long past when we could say, 'if we leave the world alone it will leave us alone'. It won't.

And then it occurred to me that in a sense we have been here before. This is the second time in a little over ten years that the British and Americans have gone to war in a desert. The difference is that, unlike the Gulf, this is a desert with millions of people living in it; and among them are the soldiers of the jihad, who will not be minded to throw down their arms in the face of superior firepower.

Time to think anew and act anew – to disenthral ourselves.

Martin Bell

We're All in this Together Now

The terrible events of September 11 fulfilled many predictions about the nature of future conflict. For years, experts had been suggesting that if we were to face some form of attack in future, it would probably not be by other nation states, but by 'non-state actors', flitting like shadows across physical borders or, now, ghostlike through cyberspace. They might be 'super-terrorists' using weapons of mass destruction – nuclear, biological or chemical. Future conflict would no longer be between broadly symmetric armed forces, arrayed across the landscape in similar ways, using broadly similar technology and tactics. Whatever differences there might be between them in numbers and quality, these ponderous military organisms had still been designed, trained and equipped to fight mirror images of themselves. Instead, future conflict would be 'asymmetric', with the protagonists using very different means to achieve very different ends.

In all this, the 'experts' were right. Tragically, their discourses were not precise enough to prevent what they had foretold. The attack on New York City's World Trade Center, in particular, released as much energy as a small nuclear weapon. Not for nothing was the base of the World Trade Center dubbed 'Ground Zero' – a phrase borrowed from the arcane theology of nuclear strategy. All the military power of the United States – its thousands of nuclear warheads, its carrier battle groups, its armed forces prepared to operate on the digital battlefield – was powerless to prevent the crudest of attacks. The West's own technology – airliners, tall buildings – was turned against it by determined men armed only with knives, working, maybe, in loose affiliation with an elusive controller. The attacks were blamed on a 'non-state actor', Osama bin Laden, who does appear to be the culprit. The United States has been unable to find, never mind hit, that non-state actor, it has attacked the benighted country where he is believed to be concealed, like James Elroy Flecker's prophet, 'guarded, in a cave'.

But the response to this tragedy needs to be different and asymmetric as well. There are signs that, so far, it has not been. Initially, the United States was more cautious than some of us feared it might be. There was no initial fusillade of cruise missiles, which would have achieved nothing. American and British politicians and senior military officers stressed that the military action was only a small part of the overall response. Wise counsel seemed to have prevailed. But on October 7 the bombing began. They did it in the same old way. The way they did it in the Gulf. The way they did it in Yugoslavia. First of all, take out the air defences. Then take out the command and control. And then? Take out ghosts? Take out shadows?

The lesson is clear to anyone who wants to see. The

required response to the events of September 11 is not primarily a military one. The right response mirrors something that has been happening in the aftermath of conflict around the world. When armies, navies and air forces work together, we call it 'joint'. When many nations work together, we call it 'combined'. And when many different agencies work together, we call it 'integrated' – multi-agency.

The response to September 11 involved, initially, the fire service and medical agencies. It involved police and criminal investigators, the FBI and other intelligence services, and their work continues. It involves airline security. It involves diplomats. It involves financial institutions, traditionally loath to reveal details of accounts, in tracking down suspected terrorist funds. As fear spread of an armed response against Afghanistan – and none of the perpetrators of the September 11 atrocities, it must be remembered, was Afghan – the refugee crisis in Afghanistan, already dire after twenty years of war and three of famine, became worse. This, in turn, brought in international organizations like the United Nations Commission for Refugees; national donors, like USAID and the United Kingdom's Department for International Development; the non-governmental organizations like the International Red Cross, Oxfam, Médecins Sans Frontières and War Child, to whom the royalties of this book will be donated.

As a gesture, the US Air Force has been dropping aid to some areas of Afghanistan, while bombing others. The Taliban government, it has been reported, has burned some of the aid, while the United States has bombed other aid supplies by mistake. It is not a good start and the former American action violates one key principle in the aid business. If you mix food and fire-power, blankets and bombs, baby milk and bullets, you risk compromising the wider aid effort. Aid workers may need to work with the military. But if their work becomes too closely identified with the military, they will lose their impartiality, at least while bombing is still going on. They will become part of the war, and therefore even more vulnerable.

But what of the most important component, the people of Afghanistan itself? The people whom the United States and its allies are trying to persuade to hand over the prime suspect and change their form of government. Will they be persuaded?

We had already begun to learn these lessons in the peace-building operations underway in Africa and south-east Europe. General Sir Mike Jackson, who commanded the force that went into Kosovo in 1999, compared such an integrated, multi-agency force to a rope. The combined strength of the strands exceeded the sum of the strands individually. In post-conflict, peace-building situations, the military forms a strand of this rope, but only one. Once the security framework is established, police are needed more than soldiers. And courts. And an independent judiciary. And prisons. We can begin to draw the rope. A red strand for the soldiers, black for the judges, dark blue for police. The inter-national organizations, perhaps a light blue strand, the colour of the United Nations. The non-governmental organizations silver, for they operate using the money they raise. The national donors gold, for they donate money.

Most important, are the people of the country, the local authorities and the ordinary people. They run down the middle of the rope, and all the other strands touch them.

It is important that no one strand is too thick because that distorts the rope, and makes it burn those who hold it. The military, which has the advantages of a coherent structure and centralized communications, is sometimes impatient and dismissive of the other strands of the rope. They, conversely, are resentful at what may be seen as the military's desire to run everything.

But this tension may be creative. In all the peacekeeping and peace-building operations I have witnessed I have been deeply moved by how soldiers take to humanitarian operations. There is a view in certain quarters that 'peacekeeping is for wimps'. Not true. The 'peacekeeping is for wimps' view has been supported by the performance of some armies which have specialized in peacekeeping and humanitarian operations at the expense of basic military skills. Others – notably the Americans – take a very gung-ho view and, partly out of concern about casualties, and partly for cultural reasons, do not interact with the local community. This causes the rope to fray.

But all the evidence indicates that the most effective peacekeepers are hard, well-trained, disciplined professional soldiers. Nobody with any sense would say that the Royal Marines are 'wimps'. Yet in Kosovo the Marines threw themselves enthusiastically into helping

War Child build children's playgrounds as part of the general drive to establish normality after the conflict there. When older youths started vandalizing the playgrounds, the Marines, with their usual brand of lateral thinking, came up with a 'hotline' so local people could alert them.

Some of those same Royal Marines may be among the specialist Arctic and mountain warfare troops likely to be deployed to Afghanistan this winter. Peacekeeping is not for wimps.

Some people may take issue with my application of the principles of peacekeeping and humanitarian operations to the wide-ranging conflict against the perpetrators of the September 11 atrocities. But I believe many of the principles we have learned about peace-building in various post-conflict operations are applicable to new-style conflict, and vice versa. Certainly, the old principles of war, starting with 'selection and maintenance of the aim', apply well to peace-building and humanitarian operations. Similarly, the integrated approach involving all agencies, which we have learned in peacekeeping and humanitarian work, can be adapted to the integrated struggle against terrorism. The conventional military may have a role, but it may not be that big.

This is where I believe we may be going wrong. The military operation may be occupying too much of our attention and too many resources. The declared aim was, initially, to dismantle the 'integrated air defence network'. The Afghans probably do not have an integrated air defence network and, even if they did, it was not responsible for the September 11 attacks. Of course, the shadowy work of the criminal investigation, the intelligence agencies and the banks is unlikely to be advertised and, even if it were, does not make good television. Planes taking off from aircraft carriers and bombs hitting targets do make good television. It may be that the military campaign is largely for public consumption, and also a deception – a distraction from other operations underway. But unfortunately it is killing innocent people. And, with no discernible success to report from the military component of the integrated operation, the media has focused on the mistakes, thus beginning to imperil the public support on which it depends. There must be another way.

My colleagues and I in the field of Defence and Security Studies are frequently asked to comment on current operations. Sometimes, we are invited to discussion programmes to put forward the case for military action. It is assumed, for understandable reasons, that my colleagues and I will take this point of view. Not always. I am a military analyst and I have seen war. But war is not always the right way to solve the problem – and never the only way. The first principle of war is selection and maintenance of the aim or, as the Americans say, the objective. What is our objective? What is bombing Afghanistan doing to attain it? I hope the governments involved know the answer.

Professional soldiers make the best peacekeepers. They are also the last people to want to go to war – again, for obvious reasons. You might think that Karl von Clausewitz (1780–1831), the pre-eminent Western military thinker and philosopher, would have been an unstinting advocate of military solutions. Not so. 'The main lines of every major strategic plan,' he wrote in a letter of 1827, 'are largely political in nature . . . According to this point of view, there can be no question of a purely military evaluation of a great strategic issue, nor of a purely military scheme to solve it.' Some may have been deluded by eleven years of one-sided military successes into thinking that war is an easy option. Most of our leaders have no experience of it. Clausewitz did, as did the Chinese philosopher-general Sun Tzu. 'Weapons,' he wrote in the fourth century BC, 'are tools of ill omen. War is a grave matter; one is apprehensive lest men embark upon it without due reflection.' And further on, the general has a surprising observation. 'To win one hundred victories in one hundred battles is not the acme of skill. To subdue the enemy without fighting is the acme of skill.' Clausewitz and Sun Tzu would have been very wary of what our leaders are doing, right now. But then, they were soldiers.

Chris Bellamy

Not in My Name

It is naive to suggest that you can fight a conventional war against terrorism. Conventional war is state-sponsored terrorism anyway. Special intelligence should locate Osama bin Laden, and whoever else is responsible for the appalling senseless tragedy of September 11, and bring them to justice, without risking the lives of innocent children through a pointless bombing campaign.

Our military resources should be deployed to escort food and aid convoys to Afghanistan, so that a population half the size of London's doesn't die this winter.

Marches, demonstrations and direct action are a waste of time, not least because the press largely ignores them. In a recent march in London, a reported 20,000 people showed up, taking up around five hours out of each of their days. This is the equivalent of at least three working lifetimes. Instead we need to re-involve ourselves in the democratic process or else risk losing it.

We have already witnessed Tony Blair's decision to support American military action in Afghanistan without a parliamentary vote. Such undemocratic action must be countered through people writing, e-mailing and phoning elected representatives to express doubts and dissent. Pressure groups should demand that the concerns of real people are represented in the senates, congresses and parliaments of the world.

Democracy can be defined as a government by the people for the people that takes into account the views of minorities. Let's stop whinging and get on with demonstrating our democratic rights, otherwise *Voices for Peace*, and other such ventures, will become a travesty of what they purport to be.

The West's handling of the current crisis fails to intelligently address the indisputable importance of human life. Our civilization is on the verge of meltdown as the powers-that-be waste huge amounts of money and resources on war: resources that could have been usefully channelled into feeding the starving and repairing our damaged planet. We are faced with a choice: kowtow to materialism, despotism and nihilism or embrace democracy, activity and solidarity. Which is it to be? It is up to us to decide and make it happen.

Katharine Hamnett

Diaries from the Front Line

Tuesday, September 25, 2001

I visited Peshawar today to recruit some workers and doctors to work in the camps. Although jobs are scarce, I used to get a lot of eager recruits to do the job, but this time people had their concerns and I found them reluctant to go inside the camps. Security was their main concern. But I still found a couple of doctors and others willing to accept the jobs.

Despite all the media hype and threats, I actually saw people of all colours and creeds roaming around in the markets and hotels, most of them journalists. One rather elderly French journalist was all set to go into Afghanistan. I tried to talk him out of it, reminding him of all the possible dangers, but he had been there before and was quite confident about the Taliban's behaviour, if 'approached appropriately'. I could not find out the meaning of appropriate approach in that context.

I met a few officials from UN agencies and refugee administration departments. They are expecting about 1.5 million people to migrate in as soon as the border opens. The figure was 7 million when the Soviets entered Afghanistan in 1979. By and large, people in the city were doing what they would be doing on a normal Tuesday.

*   *   *

Monday, October 8, 2001
Finally it has happened. Last night at around 9 p.m. I heard the news on a special bulletin on TV. Although it was expected, I had been hoping that something good would happen to avoid the whole issue, but it never did. I spent a very uncomfortable night thinking about the worst possibilities. I remembered the war of 1971 with India; I was about eight at that time but the horrors still linger in my memory. The air attacks, the sirens, the bunkers and most of all the anxiety in the family were very vivid. I strongly wished that my children would never have to live with such memories.

This morning everybody was looking up the newspapers and discussing the events. The most asked question was: 'What will happen now?' One of my friends commented that whatever may be the outcome of the war we, the Pakistanis, will be the worst affected. This is even more troubling when we realize that our nation is just an innocent bystander which happens to be in the region of a war.

Sunday, October 14, 2001
It is growing more and more frustrating now. Today is the third time I have had to cancel my visit to the refugee camps to arrange supplies of medicine, etc. This is because of increasing threats of violence in the Northwest Frontier near the Afghan border. My kids have been bombarded with so much war and terrorism talk that they now know about Osama, Bush and various warplanes.

The opinion of people varies from place to place.

Most of my medical colleagues are confused and apprehensive. One of my patients, who had been living in Kabul, has fled the city with her family and is now living here. In her own childlike way, she narrated the first night of attacks on Kabul: 'It was fire all over the skies with a lot of strange noises. I was scared.' I could see the horror in her eyes.

Wednesday, October 17, 2001
Finally today I was able to visit the refugee camp. The delay was quite frustrating because of one or another reason. There were no new faces, probably because of the closure of the border. Not many new people have been able to get into Pakistan. But a lot more are expected any day.

The aid is trickling in but, to my mind, in a very haphazard way. One of my friends, in the health department dealing with aid agencies, was really frustrated. 'How is this going to benefit any Afghanis if we cannot get ourselves out of these bureaucratic channels?' he said, while throwing a bundle of proposals on his desk. In the camp I was rather surprised to note that Afghan refugees were rather wary about the US strikes on the Taliban. I expected them to be strongly supportive of the war, being one of the most affected groups of people, but they were not. An old man remarked, 'I would never let anybody invade my homeland, whosoever it may be.'

Assad Hafeez

Nile Blues

Right there, at my feet, the Nile spreads out in a shimmering, flowing mass. The water reflects the lights of small boats, of floating restaurants, of the bridges flung across the river. From the centre rises Gezira island, on it the lit-up dome of the Opera House and the tall slim lotus of the Cairo Tower. The scene is spectacularly beautiful, and over it all hangs the thick pall Cairenes call 'the Black Cloud'. No one seems certain where it comes from. They say it's the farmers burning husks of rice in Sharqiyya province. They say it's Cairo rubbish burning in several places – two of the fires out of control. They say it's a component in the new unleaded petrol. It hangs over everything but Cairenes live with it, because – so far – they can still breathe.

'I don't know who I feel more alienated from, the Americans or the Taliban,' says Nadra. She hitches her heel to the seat of her chair, hugs her knee to her chest. 'The Americans' language is so sleazily self-laudatory.' Nadra and her American husband are photographers. He has been in San Diego for three months. She was supposed to join him on September 15 and they had planned to come back together in January. But now she can't bring herself to go. 'Do you watch CNN?' she asks. 'Should journalists collude with government? Or do the media have an agenda of their own? They're trying to frighten us all so we each stay in our little hole and don't talk to each other.' She tells me that on September 12 she received international calls from seven agencies, all working for clients in the American media. 'Go out,' they said, 'and photograph the people rejoicing in the streets.' 'But nobody's rejoicing in the streets,' she said. 'In the coffee-shops then. Photograph the people laughing and celebrating in the coffee shops.' 'People are glued to their TVs,' she told them, 'Everybody's in shock.' Still they pressed her. Eventually, she said if they wanted her photographs they could send her to Jenin (on the West Bank) and she'd photograph Israeli tanks entering the city.

That was my first night in Cairo. The city is, as usual, humming with energy. The Cairo film festival awards its special jury prize to the Iranian director Tahmina, who is in trouble in Iran for including a shot of two chador-clad women handing out communist leaflets in her film, *The Hidden Half*. The Hanager theatre workshop is showing an Egyptian *Phaedre*. The feast of the Lady Zeinab, granddaughter of the Prophet and one of the most popular members of his household, is reaching its climax with thousands of people from all over the country converging on al-Sayyida, the district which contains her mosque and bears her name. The walls of downtown Cairo are chaotic with posters for the trade union elections due to take place in a few days. The demonstrations that have so far been contained within the campuses of Cairo's five universities ebb and flow with news of Afghan civilian casualties and new Israeli incursions into Palestinian towns.

Over the next two weeks I sense a mood that is not explosive but tense, expectant. There is also puzzlement, a deep exhaustion and a cold, amused cynicism. Nobody even bothers to discuss the 'clash of civilizations' theory except to marvel that the West wastes any time on it at all. Can't they see, people ask, how much of their culture we've adopted? Practically every major work of Western literature or thought is translated into Arabic. The Cairo Opera House is home to the Cairo Symphony Orchestra and the Egyptian Ballet as well as the Arab Music Ensemble. English is taught in every school and the British Council in Cairo is the largest of their operations worldwide because of its English language courses. Yes, there are aspects of Western society that we don't like, they say, but they are the aspects that the West itself regards as problematic: widespread drug abuse, violent crime, the disintegration of the family, teenage pregnancies, lack of sense of community, rampant consumerism. What's wrong with not wanting those for ourselves?

The 'Islam versus the West' theory is dismissed by both Muslim and Christian clerics. In an interview with al-Jazeera, Sheikh Qaradawi echoes what Nadra has been saying: 'It is unfair to lump people together in one basket,' he says. 'The American people are the prisoners of their media. They're ordinary people, concerned with their daily lives, with earning a living. We must try to reach them through debate, not through hostility.' Sayed Hasan Nasrallah, secretary-general of Hizbollah warns: 'We should not deal with this war [in Afghanistan] as if it is a Christian war against Islam.'

A columnist in *al-Ahram*, the major national newspaper of Egypt, reminds readers that in 1977, when Anwar Sadat made his peace visit to Israel, the Coptic Pope, Shenuda III, insisted that no Arab Christian would visit Jerusalem until they could visit alongside the Muslims.

We are fourteen people sitting down to dinner at the Arabesque: Egyptians, Palestinian, American and Iraqi. On the table is a choice of wine, water and guava juice:

'It's sheer ignorance this equation of the East with Islam.'

'Where did Christianity come from in the first place?'

'Bethlehem, Beit Sahour, Beit Jala, all essentially Christian Palestinian towns, bombarded by the Israelis every day.'

'And where do they think we are, the twelve million Egyptian Christians, in all this?'

'And the Jews would have still been here if it hadn't been for the creation of Israel.'

One of the gravest fears in Egypt is of the threat Islamic extremism poses to the fourteen centuries of national unity between Egyptian Copts and Egyptian Muslims. The 'clash of civilizations' rhetoric coming out of the West, the transformation of Osama bin Laden from a fringe figure into a hero, the shoehorning of what people see as a political and economic conflict into a religious mould, are all appallingly dangerous for the very fabric of Egyptian society, where the two communities are so intertwined that they share all the rituals of both joy and sorrow; where Christian women visit the mosque of Sayyida Zainab to ask for needed help and Muslims visit the Church of Santa Teresa, the Rose of Lisieux, to plead for her aid.

Bush and Blair's repeated affirmations of the essential goodness of Islam are seen as so much hot air designed to appease the uneducated masses who, naturally, will never believe them. People smile as they remind you of the German propaganda asserting that 'Hajji Muhammad Hitler' was a true friend of Islam, or the rumour put about by the French 150 years earlier that Bonaparte had converted to the 'true faith'. Religion, people believe, is being used both as a smokescreen and a mobilization device. When, people ask, has Osama bin Laden ever spoken of Iraq or Palestine? Only after the bombings started. His mission, essentially, was to get the Americans out of Saudi Arabia; now he is playing the West at its own game, and the millions of aggrieved, desperate young Muslims across the world are likely to believe him.

'And what does your chap think he's up to? What's his name?' I'm asked.

'Blair?' I venture.

'Yes. Is he outbidding the Americans? He comes over here with a list of names he wants handed over and six of them are in the Sudanese cabinet.'

There is general incredulity at Tony Blair's gung-ho stance and Britain's seeming eagerness to be part of the conflict. Someone asks me what public opinion in the United Kingdom is really like. We talk about the anti-war demonstrations, reminiscent of the Suez crisis.

Returning from the Middle East after his first whirlwind visit last month, the Prime Minister seemed to think that his problem was one of communication. He has suggested that Britain needs to do more PR in the Arab world. Well, his personal efforts have been a resounding failure. Why is he rushing around with such zeal? Why does he look so pleased with himself? A cartoon in a newspaper has a flunky saying to a government minister: 'But of course there's nothing wrong with your excellency taking a second job to augment your income. Look at the British Prime Minister – he's got an extra job as PR manager for America's campaign in Afghanistan.' Blair might save the Downing Street spin doctors' efforts for internal affairs. Spin will get nowhere with people who have for a long time not trusted their governments – far less the governments of the West.

Nobody condones what is happening in Afghanistan. Anger is given more edge, yes, by the fact that it is a Muslim country, but more by the perception that the Afghan people have been used and abused for more than twenty years. Everyone is aware of the responsibility of the United States in creating the circumstances for the appearance of the Taliban, who are then pointed at as proof of the backwardness of Islam in general.

Yet Afghanistan, before the Russian invasion, was finding its own way towards modernity; otherwise, how come there are so many Afghan women professionals in the opposition camped up north?

An article in the Egyptian press maps the relationship between oil, arms and key members of the American administration. Not a conspiracy theory, rather a practical acknowledgement that 'oil, defence and politics . . . are not mutually exclusive interests'.

Nobody is surprised by this. After all, a democracy where you need millions of dollars to get into the White House is hardly likely to be free of corporate influence. But a journalist asks why America needs a pretext at all. Why paint itself into a corner with all the 'bin Laden dead or alive' rhetoric? Maybe we understand why it needs Russia and Europe on board but why the pressure on the Arab countries? Is it necessary? Several letters in *al-Ahram Weekly* suggest that not everyone thinks so. In the past five weeks the paper has received hundreds of hostile letters from Westerners – many of them taking that classical orientalist image of a penetrative relationship between West and East to contemporary levels of openess and violence.

Why does America assume conflict and confrontation with the Arab world? My aunt reminds me of the crowds that welcomed Richard Nixon, then the US president, to Egypt in 1974: 'Remember all the talk of USAID and the democratizing process and how the coops were full of American chickens? America was synonymous then with plenty, with progress and liberalization. But none of it came through.' My aunt is a doctor but right now she's lying in bed with a drip attached to her arm. Her left hand is swollen with a bad infection and a powerful antibiotic is blasting its way through her veins. Her son has had to scour Cairo and pay over the odds because the public-sector lab that produces the drug has just burned down. Next the lab will be sold at a rock-bottom price to a well-connected private investor, many of its workforce will be laid off and the medicine, when production is resumed, will be more expensive than before. This is part of the privatization process, the economic 'reforms' the country is being pushed into. 'None of it came through.' In fact, I remember wondering, when I first came in touch with USAID in 1980, why – if it was such a benevolent operation – did its officials seem so jittery? Why did they drive around in black-windowed limos? And why had their embassy been turned into a marine-guarded fortress?

Over Turkish coffee in the Café Riche, Ahmad Hamad, who works for Legal Aid (a non-government organization funded by a sister NGO in Holland) reminds me of the US-encouraged domestic policies of President Anwar Sadat. People were ready to give them a try. America was democratic and free and more fun than the dour, totalitarian Russians. But what 'democratization' amounted to was a clampdown on all left-wing, Nasserist and pan-Arab views and organizations, and eventually on all oposition. 'They nurtured the Islamists as a way of hitting the left. They created and funded Islamist organizations. They manipulated elections so that Islamists took control of the student unions and the professional syndicates. What they didn't understand was that Islamists took themselves seriously and eventually, of course, they assassinated Sadat himself.' It is the same game that the United States played in Afghanistan: to fund and aid an 'Islamist' opposition to the Russians and fail to recognize the consequences.

Since the three attacks by armed Islamist extremists on tourists in Egypt in the mid-90s, the tourist industry has become extremely sensitive. Last week some 50 per cent of its employed workers were forced to take indefinite unpaid leave. For the self-employed there is hardly any work. Entire resorts in Sinai are closed down. Around 2 million Egyptians rely directly on tourism for their livelihoods, and the worry in the country is palpable.

Practically every American, or American-influenced intervention in Egypt has been bad for every one of the 65 million Egyptians – except the few thousand who have become fabulously wealthy in the new economy. Debt-ridden farmers, disenfranchised workers, the decimated middle class, the silenced intellectuals and students – all of them will tell you they have America's influence to thank for their problems. Yes, Egyptians have internal problems with their government and inter-Arab problems with their neighbours, but these problems are made ever more intractable by American intervention. And then there's the question of Palestine.

Egyptian official media, on the whole, play down what is happening in the Palestinian territories. Egyptian television, for example, does not show the images of brutality, destruction and grief coming out of the West Bank and Gaza. Yet half of Cairo is tuned in to the al-Jazeera satellite channel. On top of every building you can see the dishes facing up towards ArabSat. And every taxi driver you talk to says: 'Isn't that terrorism what they're doing to the Palestinians?'

The Egyptian Committee for Solidarity with the Palestinian Intifada (ECSPI) formed itself in October 2000 to provide humanitarian aid to the people of the West Bank and Gaza. It now has volunteers in every city across Egypt. When I meet four of its members in a coffee shop they are shadowed by a chap from the State Security Service, who sits down at the next table. Their phones are bugged and their every move is monitored. The people I meet are two men and two women. One of the women, May, is Christian, the other, Nadia, is a Muslim in a complete veil. She tells me she used to be my student, and it turns into a joke since there's no way I can recognize her. The ECSPI volunteers go into the towns and villages to collect donations for the Palestinians. 'There isn't a house that doesn't give us something,' May tells me, 'and people have so little. We collected three tonnes of sugar half-kilo by half-kilo.'

On September 10 a long-planned petition on behalf of the Palestinian people was due to be handed in to the American Embassy in Cairo. As the delegation met in Tahrir Square it grew to some 300 people. The police surrounded it and refused to let it proceed. A group of ten was chosen and headed for the embassy, where the ambassador refused to meet them and the embassy refused to take delivery of the petition.

America's support for Israel is a dominant issue in Egyptian–American relations. I have not had a conversation in Cairo where it has not come up. When American officials talk about the lives lost in New York and Washington, about New Yorkers' inalienable right to freedom of movement, about US citizens' right to safety, a voice inside the head of every Arab will echo: 'True. And what about the Palestinians?' President Bush has spoken for the first time about a 'Palestinian state', but he has not used the word 'viable'. People remember that when the West was drumming up the coalition against Iraq it made noises about Palestine and set up the Madrid conference, resulting in the Oslo agreements, which have been disastrous for peace. They suspect a similar agenda now. Yet the hope is that if one good thing can come out of the current horrors it would be that America recognizes that a truly workable formula for a reasonably just peace has to be imposed on the Israeli–Palestinian conflict.

A few days after the failed attempt to deliver the petition, Farid Zahran, vice-chair of the organization, was abducted by State Security and vanished for three weeks. He was released only after 250 members of ECSPI and Legal Aid insisted on turning themselves in to the public attorney, signing an affidavit against themselves that they were complicit with Zahran in whatever he was accused of. 'It was a warning,' Nadra says. 'We'll let you carry on collecting medicines and stuff, but any attempt to mobilize the street and we'll come down on you hard.' This is made possible by the emergency laws operating since the assassination of Sadat in 1981 and further strengthened by anti-terrorism laws formulated in the mid-90s – essentially the same type of laws that are under discussion now both in the United States and here in the United Kingdom.

People I speak to are alarmed at the prospect of Americans giving up their civil liberties. 'It's one of the organizing principles of their society,' someone says. 'How will their society hold without it?'

An article in the Egyptian press publishes a report that Americans, apparently, are 'cocooning'. They're staying at home, hiring videos, talking to each other, visiting family and friends nearby and buying only what they need. It seems, to the Egyptian reader, like a good way to live. But the report is alarmed; two-thirds of the American economy is consumer spending, if people don't get out there to the malls the economy will collapse. People feel sorry for them. The poor Americans, they say, they're whipped out to work more and earn more, then they're whipped out to spend it; is that the freedom they're so proud of?

I walk down Sheikh Rihan with a young American graduate student who tells me that he had been approached to be interviewed on NBC. They called him for a pre-interview, he says. He kept his answers neutral, but truthful. In the end they said they'd call him back – they never did.

There is general agreement among people who have access to Western media that Americans are being kept ignorant. 'They're under media siege,' was how one journalist put it.

'Our only hope,' Nadra says, 'is to talk to them.

Sensible people everywhere should make themselves heard so that we don't personally witness the end of the world.'

A young, slim, professional woman in casual trousers and a loose shirt, the canvas bag slung over her shoulder bulging with lenses, tapes, papers and somewhere, I suppose, a comb and some lip salve. I watch her walk away from me down the avenue of flame-trees. Is the road tightening round her? Narrowing down? Or is it just my perspective?

Ahdaf Soueif

Two

And blood in torrents pour
In vain – always in vain,
For war breeds war again.

'War Song', John Davidson

The Bigger They Come,
The Harder They Fall

Still the enemy, says *The Times*. As if you can. 'The foes of democracy must face a united assault,' the paper adds, as though anyone has the least idea who makes up this prowling host or where its encampment is to be found.

'Unsheathe the terrible swift sword,' cries the *Daily Telegraph*, omitting to offer further news of the miracle weapon. 'A broad coalition of all peace-loving states must be built to defeat this enemy,' writes Ehud Barak in *The Times*, apparently unaware some of them would object to the inclusion of his own country in that list.

Spare us this nonsense.

'What happened on September 11, 2001,' even Hugo Young writes in the *Guardian*, 'changed the course of human history' and 'punctured the dream' of American isolation: 'Disengagement is not an option.' In the same paper James Rubin, former spokesman for President Clinton, declares that ground troops could be used: 'It's not retribution, it's pre-emption.'

Crush terrorism? Purge fundamentalists? Impose Pax Atlantica on a continent peppered by bandit states and religious maniacs? Spread Christian–liberal order across a savage world by force of arms? Kipling, thou should'st be living at this hour.

This is babble, dangerous babble. This is bawling nonsense. What gets into the collective head of the political class and its commentariat, shooting off their mouths at times like these? Do they think a terrorist is like a pin in a tenpin bowling alley: one down, nine to go? Do they want to give Osama bin Laden his own Bloody Sunday? Do they not know that when you kill one Osama bin Laden you sow twenty more? Playing the world's policeman is not the answer to that catastrophe in New York. Playing the world's policeman is what led to it.

September 11 is a consequence of trying to impose world order, not a wake-up call to redouble the attempt. September 11 is a demonstration of what you can never achieve with armies, spies, coalitions, conferences and international muscle, not an argument for buying more.

September 11 reminds us of another giant in history, a tower of a man brought down by a well-aimed airborne projectile from the sling of a slim young zealot. But in that case we are on the side of the zealot; in this our condolences are for the giant. Both stories would teach that the bigger they come the harder they fall. But did we not know that already? September 11 teaches us nothing we did not already know.

We know – do we not? – that the infrastructure of a modern capitalist state is essentially unguarded, and unguardable. We cannot be body-searching each other all day; we could not bar from employment any jobseeker who was Muslim because he might already be, or later become, a secret fundamentalist.

We know – do we not? – that borders cannot be sealed. Is the whole forty-year experience of Berlin insufficient to teach us that even a ruthlessly authoritarian power struggles to make an impregnable wall across one city?

From another mental compartment, curiously sealed from the echo of calls to halt the free movement of terrorists, comes a recollection that the British and French governments appear unable to seal the mouth of one tunnel just beyond our shores. What hope the land borders of Central Asia? We know – do we not? – that 40,000 NATO troops in tiny Kosovo are unable to stop KLA Albanian terrorist weapons crossing freely into Macedonia. We know – do we not? – that an imperial Britain was unable to contain so much as one terrorist uprising in little Cyprus; that we barely beat the Boers in South Africa and never beat the Mau Mau in Kenya, Jewish terrorists in Palestine or the bombers in Aden; and that Algerian terrorism wrecked much of the last century for France.

In every case the terrorists' pursuer governed the place. And we are going to have them 'stamped out' in Iraq and Afghanistan, where we do not? Dream on, Tony.

We know – do we not? – that even the watchful state can seldom find those who are determined to work unseen. In Britain we cannot so much as keep tabs on a few wretched asylum-seekers who slip away into the crowd when their applications are refused. Nor need a potential terrorist be an illegal immigrant: he may have entered lawfully, or have citizenship. We know – do we not? – we cannot keep them out and we know we cannot find them when they are in.

We know – do we not? – that with every year that passes, every thousandth link-up to the Internet, every millionth new mobile phone, it becomes less necessary for conspirators to meet physically in one place in order to conspire. The day is coming, perhaps has already come, when terrorists will not need to gather in camps. There will be no HQs to bomb, no cells to track down, no tents to ransack. The concept of 'host' country as geographical location for a terrorist group may already be too weak to bear weight, certainly too weak to justify revenge-bombing of the uninvolved. All we will be able to allege will be the 'hospitality' or 'ambiguity' shown by some governments to shadowy figures who flit in and out of their territories. The IRA, for instance, flitting in and out of America and raising funds. Shall we bomb Washington? Should we bomb Dublin? Should white supremacist South Africa have bombed London when black freedom fighters with bases here killed innocent people there? We have got a cheek – have we not? – to declare that the Americans should 'make no distinction between the perpetrators of a terrorist atrocity and the government which gives it shelter'. London and the capitals of Europe offer some of the world's best havens for terrorists and freedom fighters seeking neutral countries from which to hatch their campaigns.

For we know – do we not? – that no ghost of an international consensus will ever be reached about who are the goodies and who are the baddies in the world of violent protest. One man's terrorist is another man's freedom fighter.

Making these distinctions the grounds for invasion will sow the most monstrous sense of injustice among nations who think differently.

Of course, we must catch and disable terrorists where we can. Of course, there is a moral case for trying to snuff out those who threaten our world. There was a moral case for American policy in Vietnam. But if America failed to remove the Vietcong from South-East Asia, and if Russia cannot even remove terrorists from Chechnya and all but foundered in the attempt to subdue Afghanistan, why and how do a series of explosions in America suddenly make possible a new Pax Atlantica imposed worldwide by an American-led group of nations of which Britain now yaps to be a leading member?

It is not the case that terrorism can never be stamped out by sheer force; rather it is the case that without locating, surrounding, isolating and ruthlessly exterminating the whole group, the attempt – particularly if made by a foreign power – is likely to fail; and in failing, to energize and remotivate the cause, spreading its appeal and acting as a recruiting sergeant for its leaders. The West is in no position to trample across the East with the necessary vast manpower, firepower and local intelligence. All we would do is infuriate the Muslim world and drive moderates into the arms of extremists. That is Osama bin Laden's hope.

Instead we should ask what makes a Muslim terrorist. It is rage. Can we understand the rage? Surely we can.

Many in the Middle East, including many who are not extremists, resent American involvement there, propping up favoured states and undermining others. Few Muslims – even among those America supports – can be comfortable with this; many are angered, and a hard core are enraged.

A drawing-in of horns by the West would take the heat from this anger. After America's immediate lashing-out (and perhaps after securing the extradition of Osama bin Laden himself), I believe such a partial retrenchment may take place. And after September 11, and the horrible, horrible deaths of thousands of innocent people, one thing will be certain: the world will be the same again after all.

Matthew Parris

'William Blake Says: Every Thing that Lives is Holy'

Long live the Child
Long live the Mother and Father
Long live the People

Long live this wounded Planet
Long live the good milk of the Air
Long live the spawning Rivers and the
mothering Oceans
Long live the juice of the Grass
and all the determined greenery of the Globe

Long live the Elephants and the Sea Horses,
the Humming-Birds and the Gorillas,
the Dogs and Cats and Field-Mice –
all the surviving animals
our innocent Sisters and Brothers

Long live the Earth, deeper than all our thinking

we have done enough killing

Long live the Man
Long live the Woman
Who use both courage and compassion
Long live their Children

'To Whom It May Concern'

It is not and never has been a poem about the Vietnam War. I've never been to Vietnam. It is a poem about sitting comfortably in a safe country and sometimes wishing that the news of the murderous world would stop. It is a poem about the times when we wish to be cut off from the truth. It is a poem about the necessity for the truth.

> I was run over by the truth one day.
> Ever since the accident I've walked this way
>> So stick my legs in plaster
>> Tell me lies about Vietnam.
>
> Heard the alarm clock screaming with pain,
> Couldn't find myself so I went back to
>> sleep again
>> So fill my ears with silver
>> Stick my legs in plaster
>> Tell me lies about Vietnam.
>
> Every time I shut my eyes all I see is flames.
> Made a marble phone book and I carved
>> all the names
>> So coat my eyes with butter
>> Fill my ears with silver
>> Stick my legs in plaster
>> Tell me lies about Vietnam.
>
> I smell something burning, hope it's just
>> my brains.

Voices for Peace

They're only dropping peppermints and
   daisy-chains
   So stuff my nose with garlic
   Coat my eyes with butter
   Fill my ears with silver
   Stick my legs in plaster
   Tell me lies about Vietnam.

Where were you at the time of the crime?
Down by the Cenotaph drinking slime
   So chain my tongue with whisky
   Stuff my nose with garlic
   Coat my eyes with butter
   Fill my ears with silver
   Stick my legs in plaster
   Tell me lies about Vietnam.

You put your bombers in, you put your
   conscience out,
You take the human being and you twist
   it all about
   So scrub my skin with women
   Chain my tongue with whisky
   Stuff my nose with garlic
   Coat my eyes with butter
   Fill my ears with silver
   Stick my legs in plaster
   Tell me lies about Vietnam.

Adrian Mitchell

An Eye for an Eye

The events of September 11 were truly horrific and the resultant international outrage is understandable, especially in America. But we should fully understand why Osama bin Laden took such dramatic terrorist action against America and the Western world. We in Britain have had terrorist activities on our doorstep for more than thirty years and have not yet totally eradicated terrorism from Northern Ireland. Why, then, should we believe that we can do so in Afghanistan, a place so culturally, politically and geographically removed from our island nation?

Religious and nationalistic prejudices seem to be the root cause of most terrorist activities. Britain's ongoing diplomatic negotiations between Protestants and Catholics has helped mollify the situation in Ireland, and has significantly contributed to the decommissioning of weapons. Such negotiations and the developments they boast must be observed in our present conflict with international terrorism. America has funded and supported Israel (and also the IRA) and this has disgusted the Muslim world. There are many other aspects of the US foreign policy that, understandably, it rejects.

However, I don't believe any country can conduct a

'war' against terrorism. The 'eye for an eye' argument cannot be successful in a modern world. Such archaic views will only stimulate further racial and religious tensions. You cannot conduct a 'war' against people's deeply held beliefs. War only convinces them that their belief is correct and results in such views being even more deeply felt.

Whilst I understand that the people responsible for masterminding the events of September 11 are murderers and need to be brought to justice, I also believe that declaring war on a whole country and killing the innocents of that county can only escalate terrorism and international aggression.

The only solution is for the Christian and Jewish worlds to begin to understand the Muslim world and vice versa. They can then consider making the necessary compromises to allow them to live in peace with respect for each other's beliefs. A lot of talking must be done to achieve this.

In New York recently I saw a piece of graffiti which said, 'An eye for an eye can make everybody blind'. War is certainly not a solution where diplomacy and negotiation are options.

Terence Conran

Peace. What is that?

Peace. What is that?

Something I have taken so much for granted in all my forty-six years on our planet. I have never had to endure the suffering experienced by millions and it intrigues me how I could have managed to avoid the implications of warfare so easily.

The possibility of a completely different reality began to dawn on me one Sunday afternoon a few weeks ago in the supermarket. While trailing through the corridors of tins and packaging, I wondered what would happen if the whole system suddenly stopped? Could I take the children and flee to another country where no bombs would fall and where no deadly chemicals could reach us?

And then what?

How would we live?

What about money? With the world economy crashed, there would be no handy cashpoint in the high street. The high street might no longer exist. I wondered if perhaps I ought to withdraw some cash now and stash it safely somewhere.

Where though? Under the mattress? Far too risky. I remembered that's what people did in World War II. Yes, in easily secreted pockets. Then I realized I was being too ludicrous, too paranoid. How ridiculous. The image of a wheelbarrow piled with roubles for the price of a loaf of bread and scores of downtrodden people queuing for endless hours at the rumour of potatoes raced through my mind.

What else? What else?

No electricity; no heating; no light. Remember to stock up on candles and matches. Bad water – probably contaminated.

Food. Should we start planting now? I've never grown a thing in my life. Plants wilt when they hear me coming.

School. Well, it would probably be shut down. Wouldn't it?

Transport. Would there be any petrol?

I'm making a record but there'd be no music industry. Will anyone survive to hear this small masterpiece anyway?

And what would happen if you got ill? A toothache or sudden appendicitis? How would you get any medicine with the chemist closed and no supplies available?

A plethora of potentially irresolvable dilemmas invaded my brain.

And, of course, I haven't even mentioned the big issue.

Mainly the d-word. That terrible something that happens to us all. Don't know where, don't know when. Only, surely, not everybody all at once. Visions of Armageddon.

*   *   *

A few months ago I had an incredibly vivid and disturbing dream. I seemed to be standing outside on a bright sunny day somewhere in the City of London. Through the buildings, in the distance, I suddenly realized that a massive fireball was heading rapidly in my direction. I spun round and saw lots of people running out of the tube station in panic.

'What's happening?' I called out to the man nearest me.

'That's it! It's all over!' he said.

And I woke up instantly with my heart pounding, having just witnessed the end of the world.

How do you stop terrorism? Go to war with it?

'Come out, come out wherever you are . . . We're gonna get you!'

I'm sorry, but I just don't get it.

Annie Lennox

The Case for Collateral Repairs

Nothing symbolizes the futility of this war like the yellow ration packs drifting from American planes on to the minefields of Afghanistan. Their purpose, the US government told us, is to show that the allied forces are not attacking the Afghan people; that the war is being waged for their good as well as ours; that the United States' concern to overthrow the Taliban is matched by its concern to rescue the people from their misery. If this is so, the yellow bags could scarcely be more suggestive of political failure.

The United Nations estimates that there are 7.5 million hungry people in Afghanistan. One person requires 18 kg of food per month to survive. If the United Nations' projections are correct, and some 1.5 million people manage to leave the country, around 6 million starving people will be left behind. Afghanistan requires 580,000 tonnes of food to see its people through the winter, as well as tarpaulins, warm clothes, medicines and water supply and sanitation equipment. In the middle of winter in the Hindu Kush there is snow up to your neck. Many of these supplies, in other words, could have been delivered to the vulnerable people only if they had been brought into Afghanistan before the middle of November. Even without a war, an operation of this size would have pressed at the margins of possibility. But military action has prevented all but a fraction of the necessary supplies from entering in time.

Instead, the people of Afghanistan have been bombed with peanut butter and paper napkins, in the packs fluttering out of the sky. The US Department of Defense has announced that it possesses a total of 2 million of these bags, which it might be prepared to drop. If so, and if, miraculously, all of them reach those who need them most, they could feed 27 per cent of the starving for one day.

But some of these rations will, of course, be lost. Many, perhaps most, will be eaten by people who are not in immediate danger of starvation, as they are more mobile than the seriously hungry and better able to reach the packs. Some will remain untouched. One of the warring factions may discover that an effective means of eliminating its enemies is to remove the contents of these packs and replace them with explosives. This is just one of the problems associated with dispensing kindness at 20,000 feet: no one can be completely sure whose generosity they are about to enjoy.

The usefulness of any feeding programme, moreover, is greatly diminished if it is not carefully targeted. People in different stages of starvation require different preparations. Children, especially infants, are more vulnerable than any others. Yet all the packs being dropped on Afghanistan are identical, and all are equipped only to feed adults. The packs contain medicine as well as food, but unlike aid workers on the ground, the pilots delivering them can offer no diagnosis. This blanket prescription is likely to be either useless or dangerous.

So Western governments have terminated what may have been an effective humanitarian programme and replaced it with a futile gesture. The bombing raids, moreover, have persuaded tens of thousands to flee from their homes. Yet Afghanistan's borders with the Central Asian Republics and Pakistan were closed by order of the United States: the refugees have nowhere to go. The military strikes, the US Defense Secretary Donald Rumsfeld announced, would 'create conditions for sustained . . . humanitarian relief operations in Afghanistan'. They have, so far, done precisely the opposite.

But the real purpose of the food drops is not to feed the starving, but to *tell* them they are being fed. President Bush explained one Sunday that by means of these packages, 'the oppressed people of Afghanistan will know the generosity of America and our allies'. In fact, what they know is that gestures will not feed them because hunger brooks no tokenism.

Since the attacks on New York, many of us have argued that the only effective means of dealing with the Taliban, Osama bin Laden and al-Qaeda is through humanitarian, rather than military intervention. A vast delivery of aid, dragging the population back from the brink of famine, would show the people that, unlike the Taliban, the West is on their side. The Taliban thrive on the fear of outsiders, which, as far as Afghans are concerned, has so far been amply justified. A massive aid programme, coupled with some astute diplomatic work, would provide us the best chance of overthrowing the Taliban and capturing the suspects.

Thanks to the linkage established by both Bush and Blair between aid and ordnance (i.e. dropping both bombs and ration packets), which sounds so bold and compassionate at home, this option is now less workable than it was before the bombing began. Moreover, time is running out rapidly for the Afghan people and the chances of getting food to all who need it are diminishing by the day. Even so, it remains the only humane and intelligent approach for dealing with both the country's crisis and the West's need to free itself from terrorism.

Predictably, most mainstream commentators have written off these views as hopelessly naive and idealistic. And it's true that the success of this approach is far from assured. But there is surely no notion as naive as that which supposes that you can destroy a tactic (such as terrorism) or an idea (such as fundamentalism) by means of bombs or missile strikes or special forces. Indeed, even the Pentagon now lists its military choices under the heading AOS: All Options Stink. If military intervention succeeded in delivering up Osama bin Laden and destroying the Taliban, it's hard to see how this could fail to encourage retaliatory strikes all over the world.

Nor is it entirely clear that the attacks on Afghanistan will bring down the maniacs who govern it. Britain and the United States have been bombing Iraq for the past ten years, only to strengthen Saddam's grip. There are many in Washington who privately acknowledge that Castro's tenure has been sustained by US hostilities and embargoes. Had the United States withdrawn its forces from Guantanamo Bay, opened its markets and invested in Cuba, it would have achieved with generosity what it has never achieved with antagonism. There is plenty of evidence to suggest that, as a result of the attacks on Afghanistan, the Afghans are siding with the lesser Satan at home against the Great Satan overseas.

Conversely, Britain's Conservative government responded to the riots of the 1980s by regenerating the mauled estates until other cities complained that the only way to gain funding was to run amok. But the government had understood that while rioters may be encouraged by the residents of depressed and decaying estates, they are fiercely resisted by people whose prospects are brightening.

Some might argue that showering Afghanistan with food rather than bombs would create an incentive for further acts of terror. But Osama bin Laden has no interest in the welfare of the Afghan people. Like the Taliban, the social weapons he deploys are misery and insecurity. He seeks not peace, but war. While Western aggression has been driving Afghans into the arms of the Taliban and their guests, a coherent programme of Western aid would divide the Afghan people from the Taliban predators.

Such an aid programme would, of course, take time and it's not hard to see why the American people want instant results. But justice requires patience, and infinite justice requires infinite patience. The great advantage of this strategy is that it's safe. Far from spawning future conflicts, it is likely to defuse them. Far from immersing a new generation in hatred of the West, it's likely to inculcate a hatred of those who would deprive them of friendly contact with outsiders. Far from triggering fundamentalist uprisings all over the Muslim world, it could lead to a new understanding between cultures, even a sense of common purpose. The likes of Osama bin Laden would then have nowhere to hide. And there's an accidental by-product,which has nothing to do with the West's strategic objectives. Rather than killing thousands more civilians, we could save the lives of millions. Let's make this the era of collateral repair.

George Monbiot

The Grammar of the War on Terrorism

What really alarms me about President Bush's 'War on Terrorism' is the grammar. How do you wage war on an abstract noun? It's rather like bombing Murder.

'We're going to bomb Murder wherever it lurks,' announced President Bush. 'We are going to seek out the Murderers and the would-be Murderers wherever they are hiding and we are going to bring them to justice. We are also going to bomb any government that harbours Murderers and Murderers-to-be.'

The other thing that worries me about Bush and Blair's 'War on Terrorism' is: how will they know when they've won it?

With most wars you can say you've won when the other side is either all dead or surrenders. But how is 'Terrorism' going to surrender? It's well known, in philological circles, that it's very hard for abstract nouns to surrender. In fact it's very hard for abstract nouns to do anything at all of their own volition, and hard for even trained philologists to negotiate with them. It's difficult to find their hide-outs, useless to try and cut off their supplies or intercept their paths of communication, and it's downright impossible to try and make them give in. Abstract nouns simply aren't like that.

I'm afraid the bitter semantic truth is, you can't win against these sort of words – unless, I suppose, you get them thrown out of the Oxford English Dictionary. That would show 'em.

A nearby Professor of Ontological Semiotics (currently working on finding out what his title means) informs me that World War II was fought against an abstract noun: 'Fascism' – remember? But I point out to him that that particular abstract noun was cunningly hiding behind the very real persona of Nazi Germany. In 1945 we simply had to defeat Nazi Germany to win. In President Bush's 'War on Terrorism' there is no such solution in sight. He can say: 'We will destroy Terrorism. And make no mistake we shall win!' until the chickens come home to roost, but the statement is about as meaningful as saying: 'We shall annihilate Mockery' or 'We shall deride Persiflage'.

Actually, the very word 'Terrorism' seems to have changed its meaning over recent years. Throughout history, Terrorism has been a favourite tool of governments – one thinks, for example, of Edward III's *chevauchée* across Normandy in 1359 (or possibly one doesn't). But in its current usage, 'Terrorism' cannot be committed by a country. When the United States bombed the pharmaceutical factory in the Sudan on the mistaken advice from the CIA that it was a chemical weapons factory, *that* was not an act of Terrorism. It was pretty stupid. It probably killed thousands of sick people, by destroying their medical supplies, but it was not an 'Act of Terrorism' within the current meaning of the word, because the US government did it officially. *And* they apologized for it. That's very important. No self-respecting Terrorist ever apologizes. It's one of the few things that distinguishes legitimate governments from Terrorists.

So it was really difficult for President Bush to know whom to bomb after the World Trade Center outrage. If a country like Bermuda or New Zealand had done it then it would have been simple – he could have bombed the Bahamas and Australia. It must have been really irritating that the people who perpetrated such a horrendous catastrophe were not a nation. What's more Terrorists – unlike a country – won't keep still in one place so you can bomb them. Terrorists have this annoying habit of moving around and sometimes of even leaving the country. It's all very un-American (apart from the training, that is).

On top of all this, you really have no idea who the Terrorists are. At least I assume the CIA and the FBI had no idea who the World Trade Center Terrorists were – otherwise they'd have stopped them getting on the planes in the first place. It's in the very nature of Terrorists not to be known until they've committed their particular Act of Terrorism. Otherwise they're just plain old Tim McVeigh who lives next door, or that nice Mr Atta who's taking flying lessons.

Well, you may say, there's that not-so-nice (although rather good at propaganda) Osama bin Laden – we know he's committed Acts of Terrorism and intends to do so again. Fine. At least we know one Terrorist. But kill him and you still haven't killed Terrorism. In fact you haven't even begun to kill Terrorism. That's the trouble with declaring war on Terrorism. Being an abstract noun it cannot be defined by individuals or organizations.

Mr Bush and Mr Blair must be the first heads of state to lead their countries into a war in which they don't know who the enemy is.

So let's forget the abstract noun. Let's rename President Bush's war for him, let's call it the 'War on Terrorists' – that sounds a bit more concrete. But actually the semantics get even more obscure. What exactly does President Bush mean by 'Terrorists'? He hasn't actually defined the term for us, so we'll have to try and work out what he means from his actions.

Judging from President Bush's actions, the Terrorists who instigated the attack on the World Trade Center all live together in camps in Afghanistan. There, apparently, they've all stuck together, after their successful mission, hanging around in these 'camps' so that we can go and bomb the hell out of them. Presumably they spend the evenings playing the guitar and eating their chow around the campfire. In these 'camps', the Terrorists also engage in 'training' and stockpiling weapons, which we can obliterate with our cluster-bombs and uranium-tipped missiles. Nobody seems to have told the President that the horrors of September were perpetrated with little more than a couple of dozen knives. I suppose the United States could bomb all the stock-piles of knives in the world, but I have a sneaking feeling it's still not going to eradicate any Terrorists.

Besides, I thought the Terrorists who crashed those

planes into the World Trade Center were living in Florida and New Jersey. I thought the al-Qaeda network was operating in sixty-four countries including the United States and many European countries, which even President Bush might prefer not to bomb. But no, President Bush, the US Congress, Prime Minister Blair and pretty much the entire House of Commons are convinced that Terrorists live in Afghanistan and can be bombed from a safe distance. What we are witnessing is clearly yet another example of a word changing its meaning.

It's often said that 'in War the first casualty is Grammar'. President Bush's 'War on Terrorism' is no exception. Statements no longer mean what they used to mean. For example, people keep saying to me: 'We've got to carry on as normal.' What are they talking about? The World Trade Center has been destroyed with the loss of thousands of lives and the United States and the United Kingdom are currently bombing Afghanistan. That doesn't sound like a definition of 'normal' to me. Why should we pretend that it is?

And what is meant by: 'We mustn't give in to the Terrorists'? We gave in to the Terrorists the moment the first bombs fell on Afghanistan, and the instigators of September 11 must have been popping the corks on their non-alcoholic champagne (I speak metaphorically of course). They have successfully provoked the United States into attacking yet another poor country it didn't previously know much about, thereby creating genuine revulsion throughout the Arab world, ensuring that Islam is destabilized and

that support swings in favour of the Islamic fundamentalists. Words have become devalued, some have
changed their meaning and the philologists can only
shake their heads and wonder whether it isn't all just
a huge grammatical mess.

Terry Jones

First Writing Since

1.

there have been no words
i have not written one word.
no poetry in the ashes south of canal street.
no prose in the refrigerated trucks driving debris
    and dna.
not one word.
today is a week, and seven is of heavens, gods,
    science.
evident out my kitchen window is an abstract
    reality.
sky where once was steel.
smoke where once was flesh.
fire in the city air and i feared for my sister's life in
    a way never before.
and then, and now, i fear for the rest of us.
first, please god, let it be a mistake, the pilot's heart
    failed, the plane's engine died.
then, please god, let it be a nightmare, wake me
    now.
please god, after the second plane, please, don't let
    it be anyone who looks like my brothers.

i do not know how bad a life has to break in order
    to kill.
i have never been so hungry that i willed hunger.
i have never been so angry as to want to control
    a gun over a pen.
not really.
even as a woman, as a palestinian, as a broken
    human being.
never this broken.
more than ever, i believe there is no difference.
the most privileged nation, most americans do not
    know the difference between indians, afghanis,
    syrians, muslims, sikhs, hindus.
more than ever, there is no difference.

2.
thank you korea for kimchi and bibim bob, and
    corn tea and the genteel smiles of the wait staff
    at wonjo.
smiles never revealing the heat of the food or how
    tired they must be working long midtown shifts.

thank you korea, for the belly craving that brought
    me into the city late the night before and
    diverted my daily train ride into the world trade
    center.
there are plenty of thank-yous in ny right now.
thank you for my lazy procrastinating late arse.
thank you to the germs that had me call in sick.

thank you, my attitude, you had me fired the week
   before.
thank you for the train that never came, the rude
   nyer who stole my cab going downtown.
thank you for the sense my mama gave me to run.
thank you for my legs, my eyes, my life.

3.
the dead are called lost and their families hold up
   shaky printouts in front of us through screens
   smoked up.
we are looking for iris, mother of three.
please call with any information.
we are searching for priti, last seen on the 103rd
   floor.
she was talking to her husband on the phone and
   the line went.
please help us find george, also known as adel.
his family is waiting for him with his favourite
   meal.
i am looking for my son, who was delivering coffee.
i am looking for my sister girl, she started her job
   on monday.
i am looking for peace.
i am looking for mercy.
i am looking for evidence of compassion.
any evidence of life.
i am looking for life.

4.

ricardo on the radio said in his accent thick as
    yucca, 'i will feel so much better when the first
    bombs drop over there. and my friends feel the
    same way.'
on my block, a woman was crying in a car parked
    and stranded in hurt.
i offered comfort, extended a hand she did not see
    before she said, 'we're gonna burn them so bad, i
    swear, so bad.'
my hand went to my head and my head went to
    the numbers within it of the dead iraqi children,
    the dead in nicaragua.
the dead in rwanda who had to vie with fake sport
    wrestling for america's attention.
yet when people sent e-mails saying, this was bound
    to happen, let's not forget u.s. transgressions, for
    half a second i felt resentful.
hold up with that, cause i live here, these are my
    friends and fam, and it could have been me in
    those buildings, and we're not bad people, do not
    support america's bullying.
can i just have a half second to feel bad?
if i can find through this exhaust people who were
    left behind to mourn and to resist mass murder, i
    might be all right.
thank you to the woman who saw me brinking my
    cool and blinking back tears.
she opened her arms before she asked 'do you want
    a hug?'
a big white woman, and her embrace was the

kind only people with the warmth of flesh
can offer.
i wasn't about to say no to any comfort.
'my brother's in the navy,' i said. 'and we're arabs.'
'wow, you got double trouble.'
word.

5.

one more person ask me if i knew the hijackers.
one more motherfucker ask me what navy my
brother is in.
one more person assume no arabs or muslims were
killed.
one more person assume they know me, or that i
represent a people.
or that a people represent an evil.
or that evil is as simple as a flag and words on a
page.
we did not vilify all white men when mcveigh
bombed oklahoma.
america did not give out his family's addresses or
where he went to church.
or blame the bible or pat robertson.
and when the networks air footage of palestinians
dancing in the street, there is no apology that
these images are over a decade old.
that hungry children are bribed with sweets that turn
their teeth brown.
that correspondents edit images.

that archives are there to facilitate lazy and
    inaccurate journalism.
and when we talk about holy books and hooded
    men and death, why do we never mention the
    kkk?
if there are any people on earth who understand how
    new york is feeling right now, they are in the west
    bank and the gaza strip.

6.
today it is ten days.
last night bush waged war on a man once openly
    funded by the cia.
i do not know who is responsible.
read too many books, know too many people to
    believe what i am told.
i don't give a fuck about bin laden.
his vision of the world does not include me or those
    i love.
and petitions have been going around for years
    trying to get the u.s. sponsored taliban out of
    power.
shit is complicated, and i don't know what to think.
but i know for sure who will pay.
in the world, it will be women, mostly coloured and
    poor.
women will have to bury children, and support
    themselves through grief.
'either you are with us, or with the terrorists' –

meaning keep your people under control and your
resistance censored.
meaning we got the loot and the nukes.
in america, it will be those amongst us who refuse
blanket attacks on the shivering.
those of us who work towards social justice, in
support of civil liberties, in opposition to hateful
foreign policies.
i have never felt less american and more new yorker,
particularly brooklyn, than these past days.
the stars and stripes on all these cars and apartment
windows represent the dead as citizens first, not
family members, not lovers.
i feel like my skin is real thin and that my eyes are
only going to get darker.
the future holds little light.

my baby brother is a man now, and on alert, and
praying five times a day that the orders he will
take in a few days' time are righteous and will not
weigh his soul down from the afterlife he deserves.
both my brothers – my heart stops when i try to
pray – not a beat to disturb my fear.
one a rock god, the other a sergeant, and both
palestinian, practising muslims, gentle men. both
born in brooklyn and their faces are of the
archetypal arab man, all eyelashes and nose and
beautiful colour and stubborn hair.
what will their lives be like now?
over there is over here.

7.

all day, across the river, the smell of burning rubber
  and limbs floats through.
the sirens have stopped now.
the advertisers are back on the air.
the rescue workers are traumatized.
the skyline is brought back to human size.
no longer taunting the gods with its height.
i have not cried at all while writing this.
i cried when i saw those buildings collapse on
  themselves like a broken heart.
i have never owned pain that needs to spread
  like that.
and i cry daily that my brothers return to our
  mother safe and whole.
there is no poetry in this.
there are causes and effects.
there are symbols and ideologies.
mad conspiracy here, and information we will
  never know.
there is death here, and there are promises of more.
there is life here.
anyone reading this is breathing, maybe hurting, but
  breathing for sure.
and if there is any light to come, it will shine from
  the eyes of those who look for peace and justice
  after the rubble and rhetoric are cleared and the
  phoenix has risen.
affirm life.
affirm life.

Voices for Peace

we got to carry each other now.
you are either with life, or against it.
affirm life.

Suheir Hammad

Where does the Bombing Stop?

New York is very important to me. It was where, in the 60s, I did my growing up and where I met my husband. Our courtship took place up the highest buildings we could find. Of course the World Trade Center wasn't opened until 1973 so that had to wait till we had a child or two who whooped their way to the top. Manhattan wound its way into my heart as an old friend or close relation and, although I return much less often now, it's the only other city, apart from London, where I could imagine myself living. My first novel was set there. My newest novel tells the story of three women: one of them is Chicago born who becomes a doctor in New York.

Like so many people linked by television around the world, I watched the second airplane crash into the World Trade Center and then stared with mesmerized horror as the tragedy unfolded. I spent that terrible afternoon with a friend who feared for the safety of her son in Washington. I will never forget the images that were projected into our safe little Notting Hill Gate flat. No reminder will ever be needed, however much time passes.

As soon as I could take in the disaster which had

115

not, in any obvious sense, affected me personally, I realized I must touch base in New York, pay a bit of homage in its time of trouble for what it has given me. So my ticket is booked and I'll spend that wonderful celebration of Thanksgiving with close friends in Manhattan.

I write the above at some length to explain that my attitude to what has followed September 11 does not show a lack of feeling for what America has suffered. Nevertheless, almost immediately, I felt a dreadful anxiety that the US response would not mitigate the tragedy but increase it. The use of the word 'war' by President Bush and others seemed unreal and therefore dangerous. War against whom? Many others, I know, shared the same fear that the US response would be a wild bellow of rage, expressed by immediate and thoughtless action. This anxiety was made worse by our Prime Minister (for whom I voted) declaring total support for whatever Bush and his administration planned.

It seemed tasteless and unsympathetic to contradict Tony Blair's statement that the whole free world had been attacked. The obvious truth, that America, in particular, had been attacked for her role in various Arab countries, including, of course their support of Israel, and, more generally, for her perceived veneration of the great god Capitalism, could not be stated without feeling traitorous to our stricken friends across the Atlantic.

Also, one could hardly avoid a feeling that common justice, if one could leave out emotions, demanded that something should be done in retaliation for so many deaths. In this situation, it was a relief when no instantaneous military action took place. It was a further relief when 'the war' became 'the war against terrorism'. War was being used in a much wider sense than usual, as one might speak about 'war against drugs'. Using that sense, it seemed that our political leaders, with Blair at the helm of those European countries canvassed for support, were taking a properly moral and sensibly statesmanlike line. As support was requested in countries, such as Syria and the all-important Pakistan, it seemed that the all-powerful United States had entered a new era in which they recognized the importance of co-operation with other countries.

When the bombing started, this changed. At first, the arguments in its favour seemed fairly clear. The American people simply would not stand for a government that, in their eyes, did nothing after such a horrific violation of their lives. Anti-terrorist activity had to be seen to be believed. Many people, when I expressed opposition to the bombing, asked me 'Well, what would you do then?' This has never seemed sound reasoning. You don't spend weeks bombing a poor and suffering country because you can't think what else to do. There is no justification for a war founded on such thinking – if, as we are told, we are now at war.

Tony Blair often uses the Kosovo analogy to point out that doubters then would have halted the bombing which led to the overthrow of the Milosevic regime. I do not accept this argument, as it happens, but I note that, during those bombing raids, the word 'war' was never used. So why are we at war now? It seems to be an effort to encourage the British public into believing that we are under threat in order to stimulate greater support for the bombing.

If so, this behaviour is very odd from a government whose duty, one would have thought, was to keep their countrymen confident, if vigilant. During the worst of the IRA bombing campaigns in London, every effort was made to downplay their effect. As I remember very well, there would on occasion be an explosion which hardly made the news. Fear was not considered a proper tool in the running of a country.

I was born during World War II and, as a baby in Oxford, can remember almost nothing about it. But, growing up in London where bomb craters lingered on for years, and entertained by a decade of war films, I was perhaps inoculated from the kind of panic to which some people now seem rather proud of confessing. Of course, if we are at war, then fear is a proper reaction. But a mother fleeing from American bombs in Afghanistan might find it rather hard to understand.

The real problem, I believe, is that we are not clear about the objectives of the military action. I have always understood that a just war needs, as one of its principles, a reasonable chance of success. But the first stated aim of the action was to catch Osama bin Laden which, perfectly clearly, had less than a reasonable chance. The second aim, to bring down the Taliban, possibly has more chance, although there is no particular sign of it as I write today. If a war is not just, it is not war, it is something else – maybe revenge.

We cannot really know what is happening in

Afghanistan. Perhaps by the time this is published, the Taliban will have fallen and a respectable government will be found to rule in their place. Perhaps our extraordinarily brave soldiers will capture Osama bin Laden. Capture or kill. But that's another argument. If that happens, like Kosovo, military force will have been deemed a success.

So where does it stop? It is estimated that six thousand innocents died in New York and Washington. How many more must die to pay for their loss? Should we be bombing with our hearts or our heads?

Is bombing the Taliban and the downtrodden citizens the way to defeat terrorism? Judging by the reaction from various interested parties round the world, it seems hardly likely. On the contrary, it may be just the way to encourage further outrages as terrible as the World Trade Center attacks. So where does the bombing stop?

As my 95-year-old mother, acclaimed biographer of that great general, the Duke of Wellington, put it to me: 'When human beings try to effect just retribution, it almost always picks up injustice along the way. I'm very keen on the idea of justice but I think in the present situation military action is far more likely to prolong violence rather than produce peace. So I would advocate some just, non-violent retribution.'

These are clearly not fighting words, although my mother is no pacifist. Yet it is interesting that just a few days ago, our former Chief of the Defence Staff, General, the Lord Guthrie, writing about Wellington, in his estimation the greatest British soldier, noted that one of his strengths was in knowing when *not* to fight a battle, however tempting. It seems this is a lesson not learnt by our present leadership.

A final image that gives me hope is of Westminster Cathedral's Choir School flying back to London from a tour of America on the eve of All Saints Day (Hallowe'en). The choir is composed of boys aged between eight and twelve whose parents had resisted panicking and sent them across the Atlantic. The pilot realized they would pass over the graveyard of the World Trade Center, so asked them a favour. The plane flew over that place of misery with young voices singing *Our Father*.

Rachel Billington

First Betrayal

I've lived my whole life in New York, and this in and of itself makes it a rarity that I visited the observation deck, a major tourist attraction of the World Trade Center, in August, just a month before the towers were destroyed. I'd taken two Italian tourists there at approximately 9.00 in the morning. The weather that day was as glorious as it would be on September 11, as it has remained since for the most part throughout the autumn, a meteorological mockery of the terrible events forthcoming: the escalation of war and our continued bereavement over the more than several thousand dead. But on what would be my last visit to that renowned vantage point, I contemplated the grandeur of the skyline to the north, and then the adjacent glass and metal twin of the tower on which I stood, able to marvel at the extraordinary feat of design and architecture that raised them so high. At the very back of my mind was the sense that some people in the world saw these twins as Babel towers.

After all, the first bombing of the World Trade Center on a frigid snowy February morning in 1993 actually occurred while I was riding the subway en route to one of the twin buildings. Shortly after the explosion, and even before the rescue units mobilized, I surfaced into the concourse of shops, which have now been crushed under tons of rubble. These thoroughfares, normally glutted with people, were a deserted, smoke-filled netherworld. Sensing that something potentially catastrophic had happened, but maintaining the dead calm that many of the recent survivors have described, I broke into a trot and jogged towards the nearest exit, where an entering phalanx of firefighters yelled at me to leave the building.

My two Italian friends had never been up in a skyscraper before, much less one of the tallest in the world. Exuberant as small children, they handed me their camera and, making burlesque gleeful faces, balanced on one foot as though they were falling off the observation deck while I took pictures of them against the crystalline skyline. Then we went down to the plaza where they sprawled on the benches in the sun and I clicked away more photos. It was their first visit to America.

'You Americans, you have such big hearts,' these friends remarked to me later that day. With any sophisticated European invariably comes their world-weary view of our culture. 'You do care about your fellow man, you have more charities than any other country, you donate all sorts of aid to the rest of the suffering world. But then you are so obsessed with youth and beauty, you are so competitive. You want not just to be rich or famous, but the richest, the most famous. And being the world's cultural leader you set the stage for the rest of us. Why do you Americans go through life at such a fast pace?' one of my Italian friends asked shyly and then turned philosophical. 'Perhaps it's because in modern times you've never been occupied by a foreign power, never feared annihilation the way we did during World War II, never had your cities attacked and bombed, your citizens killed in the streets. These are humbling things. They make you want to stop, take stock of life, to take the time for a three-hour lunch.' And then she laughed.

A few days before the attack on the World Trade Center I was sitting in a church just outside of Boston watching a friend of mine, a 34-year-old bride, walking down the aisle. People had travelled from all over the world to her wedding, including a handful of friends from California. Three days later some of these wedding guests, confirmed on one of the California-bound flights that crashed into the World Trade Center, decided at the last minute to go home a day early. In the midst of the wedding procession, I found myself scrolling back six weeks earlier in the summer when I was witnessing a starkly different scenario. I was watching a woman I loved, as emotionally close to me as my own sister, a woman the same age as this bride, and who was an acquaintance of hers, dying in a hospital after years of suffering one cancer-related illness after another. These are the bookends of the summer, I naively told myself at that September 8 wedding: one month, a woman swathed in hospital white and tethered to oxygen hoses is fighting to breathe; the next month, a woman wearing a white dress is getting married. When I saw the bride's mother smiling, I recalled my friend's mother, the night her daughter died, keening over her lifeless body. She wept with an agonized note of grief that pierced me through and reverberates now as I think of the thousands of mothers throughout the world mourning over their missing and murdered children who lie buried in rubble at the fallen towers.

Now when I look towards what used to be the World Trade Center, the memory continuing to haunt the sky like phantom limbs, my first thought is a selfish one: no longer will I be able to site them when I go for a run through Little Italy and Chinatown, to gaze up at these particularly American monuments with the heady sense that is so much a part of the nature of New York City, a place where one can transit numerous world cultures in just a few blocks. But then I remember the admonishing words of my Italian friends, 'these are humbling things', a viewpoint emanating from a country that only sixty years ago was ruled by a fascist regime while being bombed by the Allies. Up until recently, it was far too easy for us Americans to delude ourselves into thinking that we were immune to the sorts of political troubles that brewed civil unrest and war in the rest of the world. We are caught now in this moment of anguished realization, like a young lover broken hearted by our first betrayal. While we are hardening ourselves to what may come next, even bearing wounds that will likely test our limits, so many things – our cultural supremacy, the lives of the rich and famous, our dream of the perfect life – already seem to matter less. Perhaps we've begun to understand that we live in the world rather than in America.

Joseph Olshan

11 September 2001: Firebirth

This is the moment when
The 21st century was born
When the mood of the world
Was altered and torn.
Often we wonder when time's
Change finds its visible form
When what will be the future
Horror or grace reveals its norm.
A rage beyond dreams, a rage
That has hopelessness as its cage
Where pain that makes men
Think living worse than death
Humiliation worse than hope
Despair without end
Dialogue banned by the power
Of deafness, a greater anger
Than the world has dreamed
Has impacted on the glass towers
Of the world's concentrated powers.

New fire-time was born from
The collision of unimaginable grace
And impossible fear; there ought

Voices for Peace

To be a limit to the ghosts
That we no longer hear;
Four planes create the grim
Shadow of the apocalypse here
With the dead whose death
Encompasses the globe in sorrow;
But sorrow deeper than hope
Has given birth to a war
Beyond the known scope
Of the known wars that feed
On the corpses that await
In our dreams and our eyes.
Let's prepare graves in the skies.
An eye for an eye has mad
Mathematics now; injustice
Has changed the world's liberty
Has brought from the nightmare
Of terrorism, an unsuspected tyranny.

Not listening has made our world
Encircled with fires from on high;
Below we shrink into shadows.
Below the refugees gather and die.
We have lost control of our freedoms
Surrendered our future to inflated
Vengeance in the kingdoms.
Beware the base of great sorrow.
We are losing our tomorrow.
The millennium today was born.
The dream of heights is shorn.
Towers of peace are invisible in space.

Voices for Peace

Hear the weeping of the race
Where power crushes seeds with tanks.
The dead burn silence in the banks.
Shadows and dying birds;
Flowers and murdered herds.
Here new time has begun.
Here is the firebirth of a new sun.
Strike a resonant gong.
Utopia will not burn a song.

Ben Okri

The Invisible Women

In one ward lay a woman named Dery Gul, about thirty years old, with her 10-year-old daughter, Najimu, and a baby named Hameed Ullah. The little girls have bruised and cut faces. But to understand how lucky they were you only have to look at their mother. Her face is half-covered with bandages, her arm wrapped in plaster. 'The bomb burned her eyes,' says the doctor, 'The whole right side of her body is burned.' The reason Ms Gul is so battered and her daughters so lightly injured is because she cradled them.

Richard Lloyd Parry, *Independent*,
on the victims of American bombing raids,
October 25, 2001

Even before September 11, the situation of women in Afghanistan was, not to put too fine a point on it, diabolical. They were the invisible, inaudible women. They were seen briefly in documentaries flitting through rubble-strewn cities, shrouded in grey, watching the world as through a prison grille, unable to work, unable to be educated, unable to move around without a male relation, liable to savage beatings if they showed their fingers or feet or the shape of their bodies as they walked.

As our politicians would like to forget, the power of the mujaheddin was bolstered by the West during the war with the Soviet Union. Our leaders could only support those men who joined the armed struggle by entirely ignoring their treatment of women. If the women are ignored now, the world will be adding evil to evil. For years, millions of women in Afghanistan have had little, had to look forward to in their lives but fear – and now the West is adding the threat of bombing raids.

I believe that the invisible, unheard deaths of women and children in Afghanistan will lie like a stain on the conscience of the world, and on the consciences of us lucky women in the West. We are visible, we are audible. So perhaps we have a moral duty to speak up for those invisible, inaudible women.

Already it is clear that fewer women than men in the West support the killing of innocent people. A survey of public attitudes in Britain at the end of October showed that only 19 per cent of women wanted the bombing to continue without a pause, as compared to 40 per cent of men (*Guardian*, October 30, 2001). At the very least, women who do not support this war should now find the courage to stand up and say, as Professor Robin Therkauf, who was widowed in the World Trade Center disaster, said, 'The last thing I want is for more widows and fatherless children to be created in my name.'

All wars kill people. But certain actions, certain situations, make the deaths of women and children more likely. Bombing raids on towns are always going to cause civilian deaths – any other expectation is simply ludicrous. The United States is even using indiscriminate missiles, the notorious cluster bombs, that that can kill and maim people up to 100 metres from the point of detonation. What's more, unexploded bomblets from cluster bombs sit beaneath the soil, like landmines, for years. At the end of October the United Nations Office of the Co-ordination of Humanitarian Affairs reported that cluster bombs were dropped over Herat, in western Afghanistan, and a village was littered with unexploded bomblets. These weapons are still killing one civilian a week in Kosovo (*The Times*, October 25, 2001). Human rights organizations throughout the world have called for a ban on their use. And yet they have now been used in Afghanistan, the most heavily mined country in the entire world.

But the most numerous victims of our actions will probably not be the people caught by stray or dud bombs. They will be, rather, the people caught by hunger and cold. Even before the bombing campaign began, the United Nations believed that there were 7.5 million hungry people in Afghanistan. You've probably read that figure before. But it's impossible really to imagine 7.5 million hungry people; from the viewpoint of our comfortable lives it is almost impossible to imagine even one truly hungry person.

Many of them are women and children; widows whose lives have already been broken by the evil of the Taliban and rival factions, living in desperate camps or ruined villages, seeing their last hope of survival dwindle as the expensive bombs flash in the sky. As I write, aid into Afghanistan has already been reduced to a trickle – not just because the lorries can't get across the border, but also because the food can't be delivered where it is needed or is being looted by soldiers. Already deaths from starvation are being reported by aid agencies, but of course most people who starve to death in Afghanistan will never be reported. They will die unseen, unheard in the frozen mountains.

She was a widow with five mouths to feed, her man killed by the Taliban. One of her children, a boy, had no toes. The Taliban had burnt down the house and he had been asleep inside a cot, her neighbours said. The woman did not speak for herself, only gathered her shawl around her face, and continued her lullaby. None of her children had shoes or cold weather clothes. Last winter, in this one camp, 12 miles south of the River Derya – known to the ancients as the Oxus – forty children and twenty mothers with newborn babies died. Their graves are earth mounds, a few marked by flags, on the slopes of the dust-blown hill.

John Sweeney, *Observer*, October 21, 2001

Yet we in the West are being asked to accept with an easy conscience the sufferings of millions of civilians, the majority of them women and children and old people. At the outset of almost every war in modern history, people are told that this war must be fought in order to defend the peace. This suffering is necessary, because it will lead to an end to suffering. This danger is unavoidable, in the pursuit of a safer world.

Indeed, the moral fervour of our leaders now must be more or less unmatched in recent times. And they are, at the moment, carrying the majority of their people with them. They have convinced us that after the deaths of thousands of civilians in America, it is a moral imperative that more civilians should die. They have made us believe that these deaths are just a necessary stage in the campaign against terror, after which will come peace and security for the West – not to mention the rebuilding of the Afghan state.

If we were sure that violence was the only means to such an end, I guess we would all be able to steel ourselves against the suffering of the innocent women of Afghanistan. Yes, if we were so sure, then we would look into the eyes of the children in the refugee camps, peering from our television screens, and say that their deaths were worthwhile because of the generations yet unborn who will live safer lives because of the American bombs. Then we would all read the tale of the mother burnt almost to death while cradling her children as the missiles blazed, saying to ourselves that her suffering, though regrettable, was necessary. But we should only so harden our hearts if we are certain that sending cluster bombs rocketing into villages is definitely more effective than diplomacy, sanctions, intelligence, aid, education, negotiation, bargaining, bribery and any other non-violent methods of dealing with the situation.

My husband, Tom Theurkauf, lost his life in the World Trade Center disaster. If we succumb to the understandable impulse to injure as we have been injured and in the process create even more widows and fatherless children, perhaps we will deserve what we get.

> Robin Theurkauf, widow and mother of three children, and Professor of international law

But if there is any possibility that other methods might have worked as effectively, then these deaths are as unnecessary as the deaths of the civilians in America. And then this horror should cry out to us with the same force of evil as that horror. And we should be as shocked, as grieving for those innocent people as we were for those who died the day the towers went up in smoke. We should speak in tones as outraged about their broken lives, their sobbing children, their bereaved parents. We should find our dreams as interrupted, and our waking hours as haunted, as all our nights and days were then.

There have, as always, been alternatives to war at every stage. But negotiation and diplomacy were pushed off the agenda before they could possibly have had a chance to work. When, on October 14, the Taliban's deputy prime minister proposed discussing the possibility of delivering Osama bin Laden to a neutral county, George W. Bush said, 'When I said no negotiations I meant no negotiations'. We have to ask why using any means other than violence was so quickly dismissed by our leaders.

If we are serious about destroying this terrorist group, we should have pursued every possible diplomatic path to that end before blundering into war. Certain aspects of the terrorists' support have not yet been openly discussed by American or British politicians. Consider the fact that more than half of the nineteen men who took part in the attacks on September 11 are believed to be from Saudi Arabia. But although the Saudi royal family has, over the years, channelled millions of dollars into fundamentalist groups including al-Qaeda, the American and British governments continue to support the Saudi leadership. We are ignoring the protection that al-Qaeda has received from sources far richer and more powerful than the Taliban, in order to pretend that there is no alternative to war with a poor and desperate country.

Not only do we have to wonder whether there were alternatives to war, we also have to ask if this bombing may end up being positively counter-productive. By turning Afghanistan into a graveyard we are choosing to consolidate support for extreme anti-American groups in many parts of the world. In Pakistan, the mood among many people is hardening against the West, as is shown by attacks on churches and thousands of young men flocking to the borders to fight with the Taliban. We must wonder why we are choosing action that will naturally have the paradoxical effect of strengthening an enemy that only needs a few cells of like-minded people to continue its murderous enterprise. We must ask why we have chosen to fight a sentiment – dislike of America – with the very action that will increase rather than decrease that sentiment.

> The mother of the seven dead children stood watching as the bodies of the youngsters were pulled from a smouldering building and wrapped in shrouds. 'What shall I do now? Look at their savagery,' she said. 'They killed all of my children and my husband. The whole world is responsible for this tragedy. Why are they not taking any decision to stop this?'
>
> Andrew Buncombe, *Independent*,
> on a scene described by witnesses in Kabul,
> October 29, 2001,

Giving diplomacy another chance might not have worked immediately, but bombing does not work immediately. Our leaders are asking us to prepare for a war that may be weeks, months, years long, to have courage, and to be patient. But the root of the word patient is *patior*, I suffer. Very few of us are now being asked to suffer. Rather, we are asking others, millions of others, to suffer for us.

When we heard the voices of Afghan women, we have heard voices of reason and hope. The Revolutionary Association of the Women of Afghanistan, an organization founded in 1977 to fight for women's rights, still works towards equality for women. They oppose the Taliban, and many have lost their lives in that opposition as they secretly educate women and children in defiance of the Taliban and expose the crimes of their rulers. One spokeswoman for the organization, Fatima, said in an interview, 'We are so sorry for the victims of this terrorist attack. We can understand their sorrow because we also suffered this terrorism for more than twenty-three years.' But they also oppose the American attacks on Afghanistan. 'Our people have to burn in the flame of war,' said Fatima. 'And all the doors are closed.'

Interestingly, both George Bush and Osama bin Laden have used similar language to insist that we must all now take sides. 'In this conflict, there is no neutral ground,' said Bush. 'The world is divided into two camps, the camp of the faithful, and the camp of the infidel,' said Osama bin Laden. But many women and children in Afghanistan are now caught between the two camps, and many will die there without ever being seen, or being heard.

We are condemming an attack of the US on Afghanistan, because it won't be the Taliban but our people who will be the victims.

> Fatima, spokeswoman for the
> Revolutionary Association of
> The Women of Afghanistan,
> in an interview on *salon.com*

Natasha Walter

A Time of Gifts

The patterns of human history mix decency and depravity in equal measure. We often assume, therefore, that such a fine balance of results must emerge from societies made of decent and depraved people in equal numbers. But we need to expose and celebrate the fallacy of this conclusion so that, in this moment of crisis, we may reaffirm an essential truth too easily forgotten, and regain some crucial comfort too readily forgone. Good and kind people outnumber all others by thousands to one. The tragedy of human history lies in the enormous potential for destruction in rare acts of evil, not in the high frequency of evil people. Complex systems can only be built step by step, whereas destruction requires but an instant. Thus, in what I like to call the Great Asymmetry, every spectacular incident of evil will be balanced by 10,000 acts of kindness, too often unnoted and invisible as the 'ordinary' efforts of a vast majority.

We have a duty, almost a holy responsibility, to record and honour the victorious weight of these innumerable little kindnesses, when an unprecedented act of evil so threatens to distort our perception of ordinary human behaviour. I have stood at Ground Zero, stunned by the twisted ruins of the largest human structure ever destroyed in a catastrophic moment. (I will discount the claims of a few biblical literalists for the Tower of Babel.) And I have contemplated a single day of carnage that America has not suffered since battles that still evoke passions and tears nearly 150 years later: Antietam, Gettysburg, Cold Harbor. The scene is insufferably sad, but not at all depressing. Rather, Ground Zero can only be described, in the lost meaning of a grand old word, as 'sublime', in the sense of awe inspired by solemnity.

In human terms, Ground Zero is the focal point for a vast web of bustling goodness, channelling uncountable deeds of kindness from an entire planet – the acts that must be recorded to reaffirm the overwhelming weight of human decency. The rubble of Ground Zero stands mute, while a beehive of human activity churns within, and radiates outward, as everyone makes a selfless contribution, big or tiny according to means and skills, but each of equal worth. My wife and step-daughter established a depot on Spring Street to collect and ferry needed items in short supply, including face masks and shoe pads, to the workers at Ground Zero. Word spreads like a fire of goodness and people stream in, bringing gifts from a pocketful of batteries to a $10,000 purchase of hard hats made on the spot at a local supply house and delivered right to us.

I will cite but one tiny story, among so many, to add to the count that will overwhelm the power of any terrorist's act. And by such tales, multiplied many millionfold, let those few depraved people finally understand why their vision of inspired fear cannot prevail over ordinary decency. As we left a local restaurant to make a delivery to Ground Zero late one evening, the cook gave us a shopping bag and said: 'Here's a dozen apple brown betties, our best dessert, still warm. Please give them out to the rescue workers.' How lovely, I thought, but how meaningless, except as an act of solidarity, connecting the cook to the clean-up. Still, we promised that we would make the distribution, and we put the bag of twelve apple brown betties atop several thousand face masks and shoe pads. Twelve apple brown betties into the breach. Twelve apple brown betties for thousands of workers. And then I learned something important that I should never have forgotten – and the joke turned on me. Those twelve apple brown betties went like literal hot cakes. These trivial symbols in my initial judgement turned into little drops of gold with a rainstorm of similar offerings for the stomach and soul, from children's postcards to cheers by the roadside. We gave the last one to a firefighter, an older man in a young crowd, sitting alone in utter exhaustion as he inserted one of our shoe pads. And he said, with a twinkle and a smile restored to his face: 'Thank you. This is the most lovely thing I've seen in four days – and still warm!'

Stephen Jay Gould

Three

Though leaves are many, the root is one;
Through all the lying days of my youth
I swayed my leaves and flowers in the sun;
Now I may wither into the truth.

'The Coming of Wisdom with Time',
W. B. Yeats

Collective Passion

Spectacular horror of the sort that struck New York (and to a lesser degree Washington) has ushered in a new world of unseen, unknown assailants, terror missions without political message, senseless destruction. For the residents of this wounded city, the consternation, fear and sustained sense of outrage and shock will certainly continue for a long time, as will the genuine sorrow and affliction that such carnage has cruelly imposed on so many.

The national television reporting has, of course, brought the horror of those dreadful winged juggernauts into every household, unremittingly, insistently, not always edifyingly. Most commentary has stressed, indeed magnified, the expected and the predictable in what most Americans feel: terrible loss, anger, outrage, a sense of violated vulnerability and a desire for vengeance and unrestrained retribution. There has been nothing to speak of on all the major television channels but repeated reminders of what happened, of who the terrorists were (as yet nothing proven, which hasn't prevented the accusations being reiterated hour after hour), of how America has been attacked, and so on. Beyond formulaic expressions of grief and patriotism, every politician and accredited pundit or expert has dutifully repeated how we shall not be defeated, not be deterred, not stop until terrorism is exterminated. This is a war against terrorism, everyone says, but where, on what fronts, for what concrete ends? No answers are provided, except the vague suggestion that the Middle East and Islam are what 'we' are up against, and that terrorism must be destroyed.

What is most depressing, however, is how little time is spent trying to understand America's role in the world and its direct involvement in the complex reality beyond the two coasts that have for so long kept the rest of the world extremely distant and virtually out of the average American's mind. You'd think that 'America' was a sleeping giant rather than a superpower almost constantly at war, or in some sort of conflict, all over the Islamic domains. Osama bin Laden's name and face have become so numbingly familiar to Americans as in effect to obliterate any history he and his shadowy followers might have had (for example, as useful conscripts in the jihad raised twenty years ago by the United States against the Soviet Union in Afghanistan) before they became stock symbols of everything loathsome and hateful to the collective imagination. Inevitably then, collective passions are being funnelled into a drive for war that uncannily resembles Captain Ahab in pursuit of Moby Dick, rather than what is in fact going on, an imperial power injured at home for the first time, pursuing its interests systematically in what has become a suddenly reconfigured geography of conflict, without clear borders, or visible actors.

Manichaean symbols and apocalyptic scenarios are bandied about with future consequences and rhetorical restraint thrown to the winds.

Rational understanding of the situation is what is needed now, not more drum-beating. George Bush and his team clearly want the latter, not the former. Yet to most people in the Islamic and Arab worlds, the official United States is synonymous with arrogant power, known mainly for its sanctimoniously munificent support not only of Israel but of numerous repressive Arab regimes, and its inattentiveness even to the possibility of dialogue with secular movements and people who have real grievances. Anti-Americanism in this context is not based on a hatred of modernity or technology-envy as accredited pundits like Thomas Friedman keep repeating; it is based on a narrative of concrete interventions, specific depredations and, in the cases of the Iraqi people's suffering under US-imposed sanctions and US support for the 34-year-old Israeli occupation of Palestinian territories, cruel and inhumane policies administered with a stony coldness.

Israel is now cynically exploiting the American catastrophe by intensifying its military occupation and oppression of the Palestinians. Since September 11, Israeli military forces have invaded Jenin and Jericho and have repeatedly bombed Gaza, Ramallah, Beit Sahour and Beit Jala, exacting great civilian casualties and enormous material damage. All of this, of course, is done brazenly with US weaponry and the usual lying cant about fighting terrorism. Israel's supporters in the United States have resorted to hysterical cries like 'we are all Israelis now', making the connection between the World Trade Center and Pentagon bombings and Palestinian attacks on Israel an absolute conjunction of 'world terrorism', in which Osama bin Laden and Arafat are interchangeable entities. What might have been a moment for Americans to reflect on the probable causes of what took place, which many Palestinians, Muslims and Arabs have condemned, has been turned into a huge propaganda triumph for Sharon; Palestinians are simply not equipped both to defend themselves against Israeli occupation in its ugliest and most violent forms *and* the vicious defamation of their national struggle for liberation.

Political rhetoric in the United States has overridden these things by flinging about words like 'terrorism' and 'freedom', whereas, of course, such large abstractions have mostly hidden sordid material interests, the efficacy of the oil, defence and Zionist lobbies now consolidating their hold on the entire Middle East and an age-old religious hostility to (and ignorance of) 'Islam' that takes new forms every day. The commonest thing is to get TV commentary from, run stories, hold forums, or announce studies on Islam and violence or on Arab terrorism, or any such thing, using the predictable experts (the likes of Judith Miller, Fouad Ajami and Steven Emerson) to pontificate and throw around generalities without context or real history. Why no one thinks of holding seminars on Christianity (or Judaism for that matter) and violence is probably too obvious to ask.

It is important to remember (although this is not at

all mentioned) that China will soon catch up with the United States in oil consumption, and it has become even more urgent for the United States to control both Persian Gulf and Caspian Sea oil supplies more tightly: an attack on Afghanistan, including the use of former Soviet Central Asian republics as staging grounds, therefore, consolidates a strategic arc for the United States from the Gulf to the northern oil fields that will be very difficult for anyone in the future to pry loose. As pressure on Pakistan mounts daily, we can be certain that a great deal of local instability and unrest will follow in the wake of the events of September 11.

Intellectual responsibility, however, requires a still more critical sense of the actuality. There *has* been terror, of course, and nearly every struggling modern movement at some stage has relied on terror. This was as true of Mandela's ANC as it was of all the others, Zionism included. And yet, bombing defenceless civilians with F-16s and helicopter gunships has the same structure and effect as more conventional nationalist terror. What is especially bad about all terror is when it is attached to religious and political abstractions and reductive myths that keep veering away from history and sense. This is where the secular consciousness has to step forward and try to make itself felt, whether in the United States or in the Middle East. No cause, no God, no abstract idea can justify the mass slaughter of innocents, most particularly when only a small group of people are in charge of such actions and feel themselves to represent the cause without having been elected or having a real mandate to do so.

Besides, much as it has been quarrelled over by Muslims, there isn't a single Islam: there are *Islams,* just as there are Americas. This diversity is true of all traditions, religions or nations, even though some of their adherents have futilely tried to draw boundaries around themselves and pin their creeds down neatly. Yet history is far more complex and contradictory than to be represented by demagogues who are much less representative than either their followers or opponents claim. The trouble with religious or moral fundamentalists is that, today, their primitive ideas of revolution and resistance, including a willingness to kill and be killed, seem all too easily attached to technological sophistication and what appear to be gratifying acts of horrifying symbolic savagery. (With astonishing prescience in 1907, Joseph Conrad drew the portrait of the archetypal terrorist, whom he calls laconically 'the Professor', in his novel *The Secret Agent*; this is a man whose sole concern is to perfect a detonator that will work under any circumstances and whose handiwork results in a bomb exploded by a poor boy sent, unknowingly, to destroy the Greenwich Observatory as a strike against 'pure science'.) The New York and Washington suicide bombers seem to have been middle-class, educated men, not poor refugees. Instead of getting a wise leadership that stresses education, mass mobilization and patient organization in the service of a cause, the poor and the desperate are often conned into the magical thinking and quick bloody solutions that such appalling models provide, wrapped in lying religious claptrap. This remains true in the Middle East generally, Palestine in particular, but also in the United States, surely the most religious of all countries. It is also a major failure of the class of secular intellectuals not to have redoubled their efforts to provide analysis and models to offset the undoubted sufferings of the large mass of their people, immiserated and impoverished by globalism and an unyielding militarism with scarcely anything to turn to except blind violence and vague promises of future salvation.

On the other hand, immense military and economic power such as the United States possesses is no guarantee of wisdom or moral vision, particularly when obduracy is thought of as a virtue and exceptionalism believed to be the national destiny. Sceptical and humane voices have been largely unheard in the present crisis, as 'America' girds itself for a long war to be fought somewhere out there, along with allies who have been pressed into service on very uncertain grounds and for imprecise ends. We need to step back from the imaginary thresholds that supposedly separate people from each other into supposedly clashing civilizations and re-examine the labels, reconsider the limited resources available, decide somehow to share our fates with each other as in fact cultures mostly have done, despite the bellicose cries and creeds.

'Islam' and 'the West' are simply inadequate as banners to follow blindly. Some will run behind them, of course, but for future generations to condemn themselves to prolonged war and suffering without so much as a critical pause, without looking at interdependent histories of injustice and oppression, without trying for common emancipation and mutual enlightenment seems far more wilful than necessary. Demonization of the Other is not a sufficient basis for any kind of decent politics, certainly not now when the roots of terror in injustice and misery can be addressed and the terrorists themselves easily isolated, deterred or otherwise put out of business. It takes patience and education, but is more worth the investment than still greater levels of large-scale violence and suffering. The immediate prospects are for destruction and suffering on a very large scale, with US policy-makers milking the apprehensions and anxieties of their constituencies with cynical assurance that few will attempt a counter-campaign against the inflamed patriotism and belligerent warmongering that has for a time postponed reflection, understanding, even common sense. Nevertheless, those of us with a possibility for reaching people who are willing to listen – and there are many such people, in the United States, Europe and the Middle East, at least – must try to do so as rationally and as patiently as possible.

Edward W. Said

War is Easy

On the morning of September 11 I travelled from our home in Suffolk and drove into the heart of the Lincolnshire countryside. It was a gentle autumn day and I enjoyed being alone for a while listening to music on my car radio.

The conference I was about to address was already in session when I arrived. A lecture was being given on the chilling subject of Biological and Chemical Terrorism. After lunch I was due to speak on International Terrorism. The participants were drawn from different parts of the country and had responsibility for disaster planning in their respective counties. Just as I was about to get to my feet someone came into the room and calmly announced that a plane had crashed into the World Trade Center and there was a major disaster in New York. At first I wondered if some sort of exercise was being given to the group. If so it seemed remote and somewhat far-fetched. We trooped out of the room and made our way to the gym where there were plenty of large-screen TV sets. It took but a second to realize that this was no exercise. As we were watching, one of the gym members wandered in and sat on the rowing machine. 'Do you mind turning the sound down,' he said, 'I'd like to get on with my exercise.'

We stared at him in amazement and then realized that perhaps he thought we were absorbed in watching a fictional movie. We returned to the conference room and rarely have I given a lecture that had such immediate relevance.

Travelling home I dispensed with the music and listened to the news as the full horror of the event unfolded. Back in Suffolk there was an e-mail from a friend in America. 'I think I've lost forty of my colleagues,' he wrote, 'probably more.'

There can be few people who were not surprised by the sheer scale of the attack and only the most callous could feel no sympathy for the innocent individuals caught in an event that will scar many for life. It took a day or so for the full horror of the incident to sink in. Gradually the United States homed in on a prime suspect and Osama bin Laden was identified as public enemy number one. President Bush, either in anger, ignorance or more likely a mixture of both, came out with injudicious language and spoke of a 'crusade' against terrorism. Eventually his scriptwriters got to him and his utterances improved somewhat. As Osama bin Laden, the Taliban and Afghanistan loomed into focus one hoped against hope that America would keep calm and not retaliate. Then the bombs began to drop and we were at 'war', albeit a war that hardly fitted any previous definitions given to armed conflict.

The first and most obvious question to ask is whether or not bombing Afghanistan is the best way to prevent terrorism. I would suggest it is not. In fact I would go further and say that there is a very real possibility that it will lead to further terrorist acts.

It is difficult for the average American to understand the depth of feeling there is across the developing world against the United States. Understandably, rich and powerful nations are bound to attract some degree of envy, but the feelings of many run deeper than that. Acts of terrorism are symptomatic of a far graver problem. In part it lies with the perceptions of many. Take Pakistan. There, many of the population feel used by America. They say that they were used when it suited the Americans and when they were no longer useful they were dropped. They remind us that when the battle against communism was being fought on Afghan soil the United States armed and supported the Taliban and hailed Osama bin Laden as a freedom fighter.

In the Arab world, despite the complexity of the Middle Eastern conflict, the perception of millions is that America has not been an honest broker and has been partial to Israel partly because of the Jewish vote in the United States. This may or may not be accurate but it is the perception of many and thus needs to be taken seriously.

The poor of this world lack military and economic power. Islam brings many of them together and enables them to have a feeling of belonging to a global community of faith. It is hardly surprising that in such a situation violent opportunists seek theological justification for their actions, build on the frustrations of the poor and succeed in demonstrating that the most powerful nation on earth is in fact totally vulnerable. While most Muslims will certainly deeply deplore the loss of innocent lives in New York, nevertheless there will be an underlying sympathy with the terrorists simply because they have been able to demonstrate that the poor are not completely without power. It is highly likely that every time an innocent person dies in Afghanistan as a result of Western military action, more young people will be recruited into the ranks of terrorism. The approach of the West towards Osama bin Laden has succeeded in mythologizing him to an absurd degree. He may be rich and clever but we can be sure that he is not the only rich, clever individual determined to teach the West a lesson. Whether by design or not, the West has been drawn into the inter-tribal conflict that constitutes Afghanistan. The ability of the Northern Alliance to govern more effectively than the Taliban is questionable and, should the Taliban be decimated, as seems likely at the time of writing the roots of the problem will persist.

There is no easy and simple answer to the problem of terrorism but there are ways we can begin to deal with the root of the problem. First, the root issues of poverty and injustice have to be addressed. America must enter into responsible dialogue with the Arab League, Islamic nations and the developing world in general. They must be assisted in partnership to deal with some of the problems that cripple their development. Global companies, rightly or wrongly, are seen as ruthless exploiters of the poor and vulnerable. They are also seen as contributing, by fair means or foul, to the massive wealth of the West. At the recent summit meetings on global trade the media gave much attention to the violence perpetrated by the demonstrators. True, the behaviour of a minority was appalling and dominated the headlines. Perhaps equal attention ought to have been given to the reasons for the protests. Injustice and the economic might of the international corporations that seem to swamp local aspiration are points that spring to mind. It is only by removing the justification for terrorist acts that terrorism can eventually be reduced.

President Bush has already indicated in a telephone conversation with the King of Morocco that the United States might well reconsider its attitude to the UN resolutions referring to Israel and Palestine. The complexity of that situation is formidable and it is by constantly using justice as a baseline that progress can be made. If it is true that the CIA have now been given a 'licence to kill' in respect of Osama bin Laden then the consequences of this action are terrifying. What right will the United States have to speak out against any other nation that adopts a similar action in respect of individuals they regard as terrorists? Without a doubt America has to review its whole attitude to the United Nations and to international law. America must be clear in its commitment to the United Nations. Certainly reform is needed in that body but effective reform can only come about when member states understand the absolute necessity for such an organization in today's world and are determined to play their full part along with their dues.

Voices for Peace

September 11 has demonstrated that clearly we need a new global order. The moral mess that passes for international affairs must be cleaned up and this will be a long, painful and difficult task. I am not without hope. The incident in New York was a tragedy and I weep for the victims. I also weep for the innocent man, woman or child in Afghanistan who will die as a result of a Western bomb paid for in part by my taxed income. However, it is possible for new hope to emerge from the ashes of despair. September 11 was indeed a wake-up call. To make war is easy. To make peace is much more difficult. Let us pray for statesmen of sufficient wisdom and stature to help us move forward into a world of justice and, hopefully, greater peace.

Terry Waite

The True, Peaceful Face of Islam

There are 1.2 billion Muslims in the world, and Islam is the world's fastest-growing religion. If the evil carnage we witnessed on September 11 was typical of the faith, and Islam truly inspired and justified such violence, its growth and the increasing presence of Muslims in both Europe and the United States would be a terrifying prospect. Fortunately, this is not the case.

The very word Islam, which means 'surrender', is related to the Arabic *salam*, or peace. When the Prophet Muhammad brought the inspired scripture known as the Koran to the Arabs in the early seventh century AD, a major part of his mission was devoted precisely to bringing an end to the kind of mass slaughter we witnessed in New York City and Washington. Pre-Islamic Arabia was caught up in a vicious cycle of warfare, in which tribe fought tribe in a pattern of vendetta and counter vendetta. Muhammad himself survived several assassination attempts, and the early Muslim community narrowly escaped extermination by the powerful city of Mecca. The Prophet had to fight a deadly war in order to survive, but as soon as he felt his people were probably safe, he devoted his attention to building up a peaceful coalition of tribes and achieved victory by an ingenious and inspiring campaign of non-violence. When he died in 632, he had almost single-handedly brought peace to war-torn Arabia.

Because the Koran was revealed in the context of an all-out war, several passages deal with the conduct of armed struggle. Warfare was a desperate business on the Arabian Peninsula. A chieftain was not expected to spare survivors after a battle, and some of the Koranic injunctions seem to share this spirit. Muslims are ordered by God to 'slay [enemies] wherever you find them' (4:89). Extremists such as Osama bin Laden like to quote such verses but do so selectively. They do not include the exhortations to peace, which in almost every case follow these more ferocious passages: 'Thus, if they let you be, and do not make war on you, and offer you peace, God does not allow you to harm them' (4:90).

In the Koran, therefore, the only permissible war is one of self-defence. Muslims may not begin hostilities (2:190). Warfare is always evil, but sometimes you have to fight in order to avoid the kind of persecution that Mecca inflicted on the Muslims (2:191; 2:217) or to preserve decent values (4:75; 22:40). The Koran quotes the Torah, the Jewish scriptures, which permits people to retaliate eye for eye, tooth for tooth, but like the Gospels, the Koran suggests that it is meritorious to forgo revenge in a spirit of charity (5:45). Hostilities must be brought to an end as quickly as possible and must cease the minute the enemy sues for peace.

Islam is not addicted to war, and jihad is not one of

its 'pillars', or essential practices. The primary meaning of the word jihad is not 'holy war' but 'struggle'. It refers to the difficult effort that is needed to put God's will into practice at every level – personal and social as well as political. A very important and much quoted tradition has Muhammad telling his companions as they go home after a battle: 'We are returning from the lesser jihad [the battle] to the greater jihad', the far more urgent and momentous task of extirpating wrongdoing from one's own society and one's own heart.

Islam did not impose itself by the sword. In a statement in which the Arabic is extremely emphatic, the Koran insists: 'There must be no coercion in matters of faith!' (2:256). Constantly Muslims are enjoined to respect Jews and Christians, the 'People of the Book', who worshipped the same God (29:46). In words quoted by Muhammad in one of his last public sermons, God tells all human beings: 'O people! We have formed you into nations and tribes so that you may know one another' (49:13) – not to conquer, convert, subjugate, revile or slaughter but to reach out towards others with intelligence and understanding.

So why the suicide bombing, the hijacking and the massacre of innocent civilians? Far from being endorsed by the Koran, this killing violates some of its most sacred precepts. But during the twentieth century the militant form of piety often known as fundamentalism erupted in every major religion as a rebellion against modernity. Every fundamentalist movement I have studied in Judaism, Christianity and Islam is convinced that liberal, secular society is determined to wipe out religion. Fighting, as they imagine, a battle for survival, fundamentalists often feel justified in ignoring the more compassionate principles of their faith. But in amplifying the more aggressive passages that exist in all our scriptures, they distort the tradition.

It would be as grave a mistake to see Osama bin Laden as an authentic representative of Islam as to consider James Kopp, the alleged killer of an abortion provider in Buffalo, NY, a typical Christian, or Barauch Goldstein, who shot twenty-nine worshippers in the Hebron mosque in 1994 and died in the attack, a true martyr of Israel. The vast majority of Muslims, who are horrified by the atrocity of September 11, must reclaim their faith from those who have so violently hijacked it.

Karen Armstrong

The Right to Judge?

> Therefore you have no excuse, O man, whoever you are, when you judge another; for in passing judgement upon him you condemn yourself, because you, the judge, are doing the very same things. – Romans 2:1

There are things we can all do to prevent repeats of the evil felt on September 11. Through increased personal responsibility we can reduce the likelihood of future attacks and so reduce the amount of destruction and pain that they cause. We might prevent them happening altogether. Our effectiveness in this will depend in part upon our understanding of the place of war and the place of blame.

We live in an imperfect world. The imperfection is not the presence of armies but the need for armies. It would be better if the Taliban would engage fully in diplomacy, if al-Qaeda would be willing to negotiate. But you cannot negotiate with 'Death to America'. And in a better world the Taliban would never have been able to take power in Afghanistan. If we were all more concerned about our neighbours' welfare then we would not have tolerated the entrenchment of this unspeakably cruel regime in the first place. But we missed that. So now we must deal with the present reality.

It will help us for the future, though, if we remember that the whole world is becoming increasingly interdependent. The political climate of *every* country affects all other countries. Who, in August 2001, would have suggested that global security could hang on the political openness of Tadjikistan and Uzbekistan? How many people recognized then that the structures of power in Pakistan are of vital interest to the entire world?

So let us be reminded that injustice anywhere is a threat to justice everywhere. If we avoid this truth then conflict becomes inevitable.

There is a wishful and dangerous fallacy about the accomplishment of peace. Very simply, we know that in Utopia there would be no war and therefore no need for soldiers or guns. And so some conclude that if we rid ourselves of soldiers and guns then that is a step in the right direction, that our world will more closely resemble Utopia. This is wrong. It is like saying that in the perfect world there would be no sickness and therefore no need for doctors and medicine. Would we make our world better then by getting rid of doctors and medicine? No. We are not in the perfect world. It is because of past wrongs, because of the faults of all of us, that we find ourselves in situations where our options are ones that will cause pain and injustice. Here we must seek the lesser of evils.

A second obstacle to us finding a solution is if we

misunderstand the place of blame, either by exonerating those who support terrorists or by heaping all the blame on America. These two mistakes are usually connected.

Although everyone I have spoken to condemns the attacks on September 11 as inexcusable, there are too many who then immediately try to excuse them, claiming that those who support terrorists have 'legitimate grievances', that they are sorely oppressed.

But what should we think of elderly men, of community leaders, who go berserk in the street, burning flags and effigies of human beings and chanting 'Death to America'? These grown men behave like this in front of children. Such acts are breathtakingly irresponsible. Is it all right to fill children with hatred because one feels a legitimate grievance?

If we think the behaviour of the fanatics is understandable then we deny their very humanity. To absolve these men, to take them out of the moral loop, to set them aside from blame, is to make them alien. They have freewill. They make choices. This is precisely what makes them human. If in some patronizing folly we wish to absolve them, we end up absolving them not of guilt but of their humanity. I think people who do this don't quite realize what a threat we are under.

If people refuse to acknowledge the terrorists' culpability this means heaping all the blame on the United States.

I think this comes partly from the commendable trait of siding with the underdog against the powerful. But virtue is not inherent in challenging the powerful. We are called to align ourselves to truth and justice, and when the cause of the powerful is good, then we should support it.

Of course, America is not perfect. Of course, America's foreign policy has caused damage. But does this alone account for the great hatred and prejudice against America? More likely it is jealousy and something even worse. As long as Europeans can blame America for the world's problems then we don't have to face our own culpability. This I think is the greatest stumbling block to informed debate on the whole subject. Intelligent and educated people across the world seem to need an excuse to avoid the truth of their own responsibility. This is moral cowardice. And the fashionable technique today for those who want to avoid responsibility is an unending tirade against the United States (a tirade which obscures their valid points).

For balance, allow the Islamic fundamentalists to be human – allow them some blame. Allow Americans to be human – give them some credit. We all saw on September 11 what America is really made of. We saw the truest nature of the American people. It is those fire and police officers who disregarded their own lives in their rush to save the lives of others. It is those men and women on the aeroplanes who did not resort in their final minutes to panic and screaming. Instead they telephoned their families to speak of their love. It is the outstanding heroism of men like Todd Beamer who overcame the hijackers on the plane brought down in Pennsylvania. It is the awesome dignity and restraint of an administration that has withstood such cruelty and hatred without lowering itself to the same. That is America. That is mankind.

So if we are not confused by the question of war, and if misplaced blame does not distract us, then we can more effectively address the solution.

We are all responsible for the state of the world.

The fact that there exists such injustice in the world, that there is such unfathomable suffering, is a consequence of the fact that every single one of us is flawed. We all do wrong, we all contribute to the world's problems. It is no excuse if we think our own wrongdoing is minor in comparison with another's.

There are terrible problems in the world: devastating occurrences of injustice, exploitation, terrorist attacks. All result from widespread instances and huge, long-term accumulations of greed, intolerance and hatred, to which we all contribute. They are not the results of isolated acts by individuals utterly steeped in these vices. Nobody is that powerful.

The problem is vice. The solution is virtue. The problem is deceit, pride, anger, greed. The solution is honesty, humility, compassion, courage.

Government has a role to play in tackling our problems. But it is a limited role. The more important part, the very thing that human beings need more than anything else in the world, is something which government cannot give. It is love.

And love is not merely a spiritual abstract; it has the most pragmatic and concrete of consequences. What does it mean to love one's neighbour? What does it mean, for example, to love a child in Afghanistan? Well, the answer is not so difficult. It means the same thing as loving our own children. Do we love our children? Well, we make sure that they do not go hungry. We tend them when they are sick. We strive to keep them safe from attack, from exploitation. And if our children are safe and well and fed, then the next thing which parents all round the world want for their children is education. Education is a powerful defence against tyranny.

It is not impossible to achieve these things but international organizations and state institutions alone cannot do it. The task is too vast. It needs to be driven by love, by individuals. It will happen when millions, billions of people put their minds and energy and resources in to making it happen. What do we have to do in life that is more important than supporting our brothers' welfare?

Our everyday actions shape the world we live in. Every person who has travelled abroad or met foreigners in the United Kingdom has affected international relations. When we travel abroad do we treat local people with respect, with kindness, with interest? A thousand tourists who do this will have a bigger impact on building up goodwill than all the diplomatic efforts of an ambassador. The Foreign Office will do everything they can to keep a strong relationship between Pakistan and the United Kingdom. But this task would be infinitely easier if every Brit who had travelled through Pakistan had treated all the locals they met with great respect and with kindness. For then it would be far more difficult for fanatics to dance in the street drawing crowds calling for death to the West. This is important. If those crowds were ever to grow unmanageable, then it is conceivable that Osama bin Laden's supporters would get their hands on nuclear bombs. Could that possibly happen because we waltz arrogantly through other people's countries utterly indifferent to their terrible poverty, wishing only to indulge our cameras, stomachs and throats without a care for local life? That is not loving our neighbour, and it breeds a deadly resentment.

Or what about at home? What if we were all more welcoming to immigrants here? What if we made more effort in helping them to integrate? Then would it not be more difficult for terrorist groups to find alienated and disaffected young men who they could brainwash with their blasphemous corruption of Islam? Maybe we cannot stop every last person from being recruited, but we can do much to reduce the support for organizations bent on terror and disorder. The stronger and deeper our relations are with the Muslim world then the more difficult it will be for terrorists to find environments of support and complicity for them to move in.

And as for war, it matters how every one of our soldiers chooses to fight. We need a military that can discriminate between Taliban soldiers and Afghan civilians. Otherwise the war is pointless and impossible. To achieve this takes incredible intelligence work, incredible science in developing sufficiently accurate ordnance and incredible dedication from pilots and crews upon whose every effort the final result depends.

Each of us, however far removed, has an effect. Our efforts can only ever be drops in the ocean, but when millions of people are willing to make that effort, then the ocean is mighty indeed.

If we want to fight against wickedness in the world, if we want to reduce the amount of evil, then there is only one place where we are guaranteed success. That is in the fight against the wickedness in our own hearts. Each of us has greed, and pride, and anger, and hatred. We can all strive to overcome these faults and there is no one in the world but ourselves who can stop us from succeeding.

To change the world, change oneself. Learn to love.

James Mawdsley

Hearts and Minds:
Avoiding a New Cold War

This is a different kind of war. That much of what we are being told, at least, is true. And because of that, a different kind of analysis is required.

The single most common question anti-war activists are confronted with is, 'What's your solution?' Although many elements of a sensible solution have been offered, the anti-war movement has reached no general consensus on the fundamentals.

In the past, activists who critiqued and/or resisted unjust US foreign policy and militarism faced three main scenarios in which US actions were blatantly unjust and the raw exercise of US power was obviously wrong:

1. US attempts to overthrow democratically elected governments, such as Iran in 1953, Guatemala in 1954, and Chile in 1973.

2. US wars against national liberation movements, such as Vietnam in the 1960s, or against attempts to consolidate national liberation, such as Nicaragua throughout the 1980s.

3. US wars in response to clearly illegal acts, but where the US short-circuited negotiations and used indiscriminate, gratuitous violence that killed huge numbers of civilians (directly and indirectly), such as in the Gulf War in 1991.

In all those cases, there was no threat to the people of the United States, even though many of the interventions were carried out in the context of the Cold War project of making people afraid of threats-that-might-come. The solutions were simple – in the first two cases, no intervention by the United States and in the third, diplomacy and negotiations within the framework of international law while keeping the United States from unilateral military action.

But this war was sparked by attacks on US soil, and people feel threatened and afraid, for understandable reasons.

In a climate of fear, it doesn't matter to many that the military strategy being pursued by the United States is immoral (the civilian death-toll from bombing and starvation resulting from the attack will no doubt reach into the tens, possibly hundreds of thousands without immediate action) and ineffective (it will most likely breed more terrorism, not end it). Americans are confronted with a genuine threat and want to feel safe again.

As a result, proposals offered by some in the anti-war movement have been difficult for the public to take seriously. It is clear that pacifism is only of interest to the few in the United States. That is not said out of disrespect for principled pacifists who consistently reject violence, but simply to point out that any political argument that sounds like 'turn the other cheek' will be ignored. It is also hard to imagine how it would have an impact on the kind of people who committed the crime against humanity on September 11.

The only public display of pacifism that would be meaningful now would be for pacifists to put their bodies on the line, to put themselves somewhere between the weapons of their government and the innocent victims in Afghanistan. Short of that, statements evoking pacifism will be worse than ineffective; they will paint all the anti-war movement as out of touch with reality.

Also inadequate are calls for terrorism to be treated solely as a police matter in which law enforcement agencies pursue the perpetrators and bring them to justice through courts, domestic or international. That is clearly central to the task but is insufficient and unrealistic; the problem of terrorist networks is a combined political and criminal matter and requires a combined solution.

So, what should those who see the futility of the current military strategy be calling for?

First, we must support the call made by UN-affiliated and private aid agencies for an immediate bombing halt to allow a resumption of the serious food distribution efforts needed to avoid a catastrophe.

There will need to be a transitional government, which should be – as has been suggested for the past decade – ethnically broad-based with a commitment to allowing international aid and basic human rights. It must, however, be under UN auspices, with the United States playing a minimal role because of its history of 'covert' action in the region. It should also be one that does not sell off Afghanistan's natural resources and desirable location for pipelines on the cheap to multi-national corporations.

While all that goes forward, the United States should do what is most obviously within its power to do, to lower the risk of further terrorist attacks: begin to change US foreign policy in a way that could win over the people of the Islamic world by acknowledging that many of their grievances – such as the sanctions on Iraq, the presence of US troops in Saudi Arabia, Israel's occupation of and aggression against Palestine – are legitimate and must be addressed.

This shouldn't be confused with 'giving in to the terrorists' or 'negotiating with Osama bin Laden'. It is neither. It is a practical strategy that demonstrates that a powerful nation can choose to correct policies that were rooted in a desire to extend its dominance over a region and its resources and are now not only unjust but untenable. It is a sign of strength, and it is the right thing to do.

Some have argued against any change in US foreign policy in the near term. International law expert Richard Falk wrote in *The Nation*, 'Whatever the global role of the United States – and it is certainly responsible for much global suffering and injustice, giving rise to widespread resentment that at its inner core fuels the terrorist impulse – it cannot be addressed so long as this movement of global terrorism is at large and prepared to carry on with its demonic work.'

In fact, the opposite is true: now is precisely the time to address these long-term issues.

Here we can actually take a page from 'liberal' counter-insurgency experts who saw that the best way to defeat movements of national liberation was to win the hearts and minds of people rather than try to defeat them militarily. In those situations, as in this one, military force simply drives more people into resistance. Measures designed to ease the pressure toward insurgency, such as land reform then and changing US Middle East policy now, are far more likely to be effective. The alternative in Vietnam was a wholesale attempt to destroy civilian society – 'draining the swamp' in Donald Rumsfeld's phrase. The alternative now would be unending global war.

In the past, such strategies were part of a foreign policy 'debate' in which the end goal of US economic domination of Third World countries was shared by all parties, and so they were entirely illegitimate. Now, it is different – these terrorists are not the voice of the dispossessed and they are not a national liberation movement. Their vision for their own societies is grotesque.

But they do share something with the wider populace of their countries.

There is tremendous justified anger in the Islamic world at US foreign policy. For the vast majority of the populace, it has not translated to anger at the United States as a nation or at Americans as a people. For groups like al-Qaeda, it has. Their aims and methods are rejected by that majority, but the shared anger at US domination provides these terror networks their only cover. A strategy to successfully 'root out' those networks must isolate them from the populace by eliminating what they hold in common. It is necessary to get the co-operation not just of governments of Islamic nations but of their people as well. The only way is to remove their sources of grievance.

These changes in policy must be preliminary to a larger change. The United States must drop its posture of the unilateralist, interventionist superpower. In lieu of its current policy of invoking the rule of law and the international community when convenient and ignoring them when it wishes, it must demonstrate a genuine commitment to being bound by that law and the will of the international community in matters of war and peace.

Many have said of the Afghans, and perhaps by extension of many other deprived peoples, 'Feed them and you'll win them over'. This attitude dehumanizes those people. Nobody will accept bombs with one hand and food with the other. Nor will anyone feel gratitude over food doled out by an arrogant superpower that insists on a constant double standard in international relations and makes peremptory demands of other nations on a regular basis. To win the support of Afghans and others for the long term, which will be necessary to substantially reduce the danger of terrorism, the United States must treat other peoples with dignity and respect. We must recognize we are simply one nation among many.

This strategy will not win over Osama bin Laden or other committed terrorists to our side; that's not the objective. Instead, we have to win over the people.

The choice we face as a nation is similar to that faced at the end of World War II. The capitalist West, the Communist world, and many of the colonies had united to defeat fascism. That could have been the basis of building an equitable world order, with the United States helping to equalize levels of wealth and consumption around the world. Had that path been taken, the world would be a far safer place today, for Americans and others.

Instead, US leaders chose the path of the Cold War, which was not so much an attempt to contain Soviet-style communism as it was to destroy any example of independent development in the Third World, to extend and entrench our economic superiority. That effort harmed democracy in our country and in others, killed millions, and has led in the end to the creation of new and terrifying threats to all our safety.

Government officials are already speaking as if we are fighting a new Cold War, with President Bush calling the war on Afghanistan 'the first battle of the war of the twenty-first century'.

We cannot let history repeat itself.

Rahul Mahajan and Robert Jensen

Real Aid, Fair Trade and
the Green Renaissance

Whether science and society like it or not the results of the human genome project proved the dream of genetic determinism to be dead. All people are members of a single species sharing 30,000 genes that code some 300,000 proteins, the stuff of life. From the moment of their inception these proteins are subject to moulding by the environment within the cell, which is itself at the mercy of the wider environment in which the person lives. The truly staggering diversity of people thus came about as the descendants of Eve began to meet the challenge of the different environments they encountered in their race across the world.

This world is now falling apart environmentally, socially and ethically. Stock exchanges, insurance companies, businesses and people, both rich and poor, are now having to grapple with the problems caused by gross disruption of climate and weather and by over-grazing, over-fishing, soil erosion, eutrophication, pollution, Aids and terror. Even the richest economies are running out of water and more and more of their farmers can no longer make a viable living. Rural communities are in disarray, while graffiti and negative equity stain suburbia as inner cities fall into decay.

There are already solutions to all environmental problems in the pipelines of research and development. Wave power, which could produce the base load of electricity needed to service a modern world of 10 billion people, would be a prime source, with solar power, offshore wind and co-generation from waste, topping up local supplies. Fuel cells could replace the pollution problems of internal combustion with pure water vapour, integrated crop management and hi-tech hydroponics to close the water and the pollution cycles. As these new technologies become integrated into the market place, millions of jobs will be created.

Across the world tens of thousands of partnerships of people and businesses, both great and small, and governance at all levels, are beginning to think globally and act locally. I like to call this mass movement of people the Green Renaissance.

The quick profiteers and green doomsayers, who resort to scaremongering, often on issues of marginal concern, either ignore the fact that an environmental awakening is forthcoming or intone that 'it is too little too late'. I agree that it is not yet happening fast enough, either for the right reasons or on a grand enough scale, but at least these grass roots stirrings are now in the public domain. It is my firm belief that when people are fired not by the divisive spirit of revolution but the spiritual reunion of a renaissance, much can be achieved. Peace must happen now because the longer we wait the more difficult it will be.

The bombing in Afghanistan must stop and the supplies of relief and aid be significantly increased. This war is one more symptom of the disparity between the haves and have nots of the world, in which at least 16,000 children die every day for want of basic health care and food and 600 die every hour for want of potable water.

To address this crisis, all the world's wilderness areas that are still in a viable state must be saved. Such areas include estuaries, sea grass beds and reefs and the fisheries that depend on them. For they are the world bank of genetic information, the only viable investment we have which will allow rehabilitation of the vast areas of the world that are in need of stabilization. The costs of buying up the logging rights on all old growth forests now under threat are miniscule compared to the downstream effects of their continued destruction.

The same common sense economics suggest that if the recommendations of the Kyoto protocol were implemented, conservation and the necessary rehabilitation of the environment could be funded through the much discussed carbon sequestration tax. This tax would create millions of jobs in the rural areas of desperately poor countries through planting and managing forests. Reforestation would stabilize soils and whole watersheds, improving local climates and downstream water supplies and fisheries, while giving the wealthy world the time to invest in alternative sources of energy as quickly as possible.

Those nations rich in fossil fuels have nothing to fear for most are also rich in alternatives. Once they stop wasting these precious resources on the production of energy then their true value as feedstock for the plasto-chemical lifestyles of the twenty-first century can be realized. The thriving recycling plastic industry may result in fossil fuel being reclassified as a 'quasi-renewable resource'.

With modern methods of satellite surveillance, all this could be monitored in the detail it deserves, as could overfishing. The immense subsidies, which are driving this industry to the wall of extinction, could then be spent putting all fish and shellfish farms on closed circuit, 'flowgro' systems thus avoiding pollution of our rivers and inshore waters. The crop could be fed on earthworms and rotifers, themselves fed on cardboard, treated grey water and other organic waste. Not on capelin and sandeel, small fishes that are crucial steps in the marine food-chain which feeds the larger fish of commerce.

Another source of funding could come from the oil companies themselves, many of which are already starting to broaden their portfolios into alternatives. At the moment pure dogma is forcing them to waste energy and landfill space through recycling redundant oil rigs at immense cost, (an estimated £22 billion for the North Sea fields alone), with no researched, let alone proven benefit to the marine environment. Surely it makes more economic sense to clean them up and make them safe? Then, artificial reefs to enhance marine life and fisheries and test rigs for wave power and hydrogen production could be developed, as is now being done in the United States. Part of the money so saved could be used to more rapidly broaden the investment base of these industries and fund other aspects of real marine conservation, which must include giving local fisheries back to local communities.

As tourism was the world's biggest industry before the events of September 11 and as it is an industry that in part depends on a rich and thriving heritage of culture, custom, cuisine, landscape, and biodiversity, it must be reconfigured as soon as possible. Nature can be seen as a great healer, teaching people to love and respect each other's ways of life amongst rich and poor alike. The increasing expenditure on gardens and gardening and the increasing popularity of botanic gardens and nature-based theme parks in the West shows that the desire to till the soil and recreate Eden here on earth is still a natural impulse.

The growing world demand for organic food, traditional medicine and fair trade artifacts are beginning to put into question the destruction of age-old crafts, customs and practices. Fair trade is already revitalizing thousands of village communities across the globe. Real aid, which recognizes and rewards intellectual property, could speed up these processes, giving the developing world the breathing space it needs to decide its own future courses of action. The dropping of food supplies in Afghanistan is good news indeed but real aid, putting village communities back into self-sufficient working order, must figure in the order of the way ahead.

It is my hope that the present crisis will catalyse a new deal for all creeds and kinds. A centre of Real Aid and Fair Trade, not rotten to the core with profit for profit's sake but a flagship of sustainable redevelopment, where local people and local environments will always call the shots, could mean that all the sorrow felt has not be in vain.

David Bellamy

The Jihad for Peace

The word Islam has the dual meaning of 'peace' and 'submission'. Islam seeks peace not just for its own sake; it is an essential precondition for and consequence of submission to the 'will of God', the creation of the circumstances in which the life of faith can be implemented in all aspects of human existence. So, why does Islam today appear to be synonymous with violence? And why are those who claim to be following the 'will of God' so bent on the path of war?

As Anwar Ibrahim, the former Deputy Prime Minister of Malaysia, asked in an article written from prison, how 'in the twenty-first century, the Muslim world could have produced a bin Laden'; or, as many supporters of Anwar, whose only crime is standing up against the corruption and despotism of Mahathir Muhammad, Malaysia's incumbent Prime Minister for the last two decades, are asking: why is the Muslim world so crammed with despots, theocrats, autocrats and dictators? Or, to put it another way: why have Muslim societies failed so spectacularly to come to terms with modernity?

These are not new questions. But after September 11, they have acquired a new poignancy and a much broader currency. However, such debate and earnest discourse has some notable features. For the most part, Muslim intellectuals and writers living and working in the West conduct the debate, though they enjoy a readership and close links within the Muslim world. The reason is not hard to find. Living in the West requires a direct response to the circumstances and human dilemmas of modernity; it allows more ready access to sources of Muslim scholarship than in most Muslim countries; within the Muslim world dissent, wide-ranging intellectual inquiry and argument has little if any public scope. So the central debate on the contemporary meaning of Islam is, in its most challenging form, doubly marginal. It occurs outside Muslim nations, where any attempt to apply its ideas is blocked by existing power structures and entrenched vested interests. In the West, as it is the concern of a minority, it is almost inaudible and invisible. Furthermore from a Western perspective it is not consistent with popular perceptions of Islam or the realpolitik of relations with the Muslim world.

Defining the predicament of modern Muslim nations and Islam in the modern world is not difficult. Ascribing reasons is an equally effortless procedure. We have tended to look to outsiders for answers to these questions. It is apparent, despite all the posturing of governments, that the fate of the Muslim world is affected and determined by decisions taken elsewhere, creating a widespread sense of dispossession and powerlessness.

Therefore, much energy goes into critique of the actions and consequences of the centres of power, the nexus of Western government, economy, industry and popular culture where modernity is manufactured and exported to its recipients in the Muslim world. For example, Muslims are quick to point out the double standards of America, both in its domestic rhetoric and foreign policy. The American support for despotic regimes, its partiality towards the Israelis and a long series of covert operations have undermined democratic movements in the Muslim world. There is truth in these assertions. But such truths cannot explain or provide all the answers. Indeed, the most significant answers lie deep within the history, social practice and intellectual and political inertia of Muslims themselves. Holding a mirror to our faults is something we Muslims are just too reluctant to do. But unless we re-examine our own assumptions, our own perceptions of what it means to be a Muslim in the twenty-first century, peace – in any meaningful sense – will continue to elude us.

The question of peace, then, is tied up with a re-examination of the meaning and nature of Islam in contemporary times. The Muslim world has no doubt that its identity is shaped by the best religion with the finest arrangements and precepts for all aspects of human existence and the most glorious of all human histories. Muslim rhetoric is shaped by the ideals of Islam where all is sacred, nothing secular and justice the paramount duty. The problem, as all concerned acknowledge, is that Muslims, as individuals and nations, are neither expressly Islamic nor all that just. The problem of flawed humanity is answered, in the deepest core of Muslim being, by the unquestionable need to be more Islamic. So, we are constantly retreating to a more and more romanticized notion of 'Islam'. Time after time, we have watched as the definition of what is 'Islamic' in contemporary times and circumstances is shrunk and reduced to pathological levels. Our most sacred concepts have been monopolized and hijacked by undereducated 'clerics', by obscurantist 'sheikhs' and 'ulama' (scholars), fanatics and madmen.

This process of reduction itself is also not new. But now it has reached such an absurd state that the very ideas that are supposed to take Muslims towards peace and prosperity are now guaranteed to take them in the opposite direction. From the subtle beauty of a perennial challenge to construct justice through mercy and compassion, we get mechanistic formulae fixated. The extremes are repeated by people convinced they have no duty to think for themselves because all questions have been answered for them by the classical ulamas, far better men long dead. And because everything carries the brand name of Islam, to question it or argue against it is tantamount to voting for sin.

Peace will elude the Muslim world as long as Muslims continue to perform violence on our own ideas and concepts. Let me illustrate the nature of this violence by looking at two very common Muslim concepts: the notions of jihad (struggle) and ijma (consensus) that shape much of Muslim identity and outlook. Jihad has now been reduced to the single meaning of 'Holy War'. This translation is perverse not only because the concept's spiritual, intellectual and social components have been stripped away, but also it has been reduced to war by any means, including terrorism. So anyone can now declare jihad on anyone, without ethical or moral rhyme or reason. Nothing could be more perverted or pathologically more distant from the initial meaning of jihad. The primary meaning of jihad is peace, not war. Peace and justice are the core values of the message of Islam. Thus war cannot, nor has it ever been, an instrument of Islam. Muslim polities have been no strangers to war, like any other societies, but conversion to Islam is unequivocally declared by the Koran and understood by the community to be a matter of private, personal conscience between each individual and God. The entire history of human experience testifies that war instigates, perpetuates and compounds all the conditions that negate justice and are not peace. War demeans the dignity of the human person, which Islam explicitly seeks to nurture and promote. Even if jihad is reduced to the sole meaning of war, it cannot be war by any or all means. The rules of engagement established by Prophet Muhammad are well known to all Muslims and the basis on which even the Taliban's clerics had to condemn the terrorist attacks in America and declare them unethical. The most central notion of Islam is tawheed, usually translated as unity of God. But this unity extends to, indeed demands, moral and ethical unity: Islam insists that there cannot be a distinction between ends and means, and that just causes must be pursued by just means.

Given the violence done to the notion of jihad, it is hardly surprising that in modern times no call for jihad has translated into securing justice for anyone, least of all those on whose behalf and in whose interests it has been proclaimed. A central principle of our faith has become an instrument of militant expediency and morally bankrupt. Those who call Muslims to jihad are dead to compassion and mercy, the most essential values by which justice and peace must and should be sought.

Similarly, the idea of ijma, the central notion of communal life in Islam, has been reduced to the consensus of a select few. Ijma literally means consensus of the people. The concept dates back to the practice of Prophet Muhammad himself as leader of the original polity of Muslims. When the Prophet Muhammad wanted to reach a decision, he would call the whole Muslim community – then, admittedly not very large – to the mosque. A discussion would ensue; arguments for and against would be presented. Finally, the entire gathering would reach a consensus. Thus, a democratic spirit was central to communal and political life in early Islam. But over time the clerics and religious scholars have removed the people from the equation – and reduced ijma to 'the consensus of the religious scholars'. Not surprisingly, authoritarianism, theocracy and despotism reign supreme in the Muslim world. The political domain finds its model in what has become the accepted practice and metier of the authoritatively 'religious' adepts, those who claim the monopoly of exposition of Islam. Obscurantist mullahs dominate Muslim societies and circumscribe them with fanaticism and absurdly reductive logic.

The way to peace requires Muslims to move in the

opposite direction: from reduction to synthesis. Ordinary Muslims around the world who have concerns, questions and considerable moral dilemmas about this current state of affairs must reclaim the basic concepts of Islam and reframe them in a broader context. Ijma must mean participatory consensus leading to participatory and accountable governance. Jihad must be understood in its complete spiritual meaning as the struggle for peace and justice as a lived reality for all people everywhere.

More specifically, we need to declare jihad for peace. In its original multidimensional meaning, jihad must involve Muslims in concerted, co-operative endeavour to combat poverty, disease, the indignity of unemployment, the lack of educational opportunity and provision, the underachievement of economic institutions, all aspects of corruption, denials of basic rights to freedom and the oppression of women – all those things that afflict Muslim societies everywhere. And this jihad has to be conducted by intellectual and moral means. When the deformed political institutions of our nations impede the process of peace and justice, we have a duty to peacefully work together to bring meaningful change based on programmes of remedial action. Jihad for peace also involves intellectual efforts for peace, including the construction of a discourse for peace. When the inequities of the global system impede our efforts to bring improvement to the needy, it becomes a matter of jihad for every Muslim to engage in dialogue and not be satisfied with self-righteous denunciation. In such a jihad, it becomes a supreme duty of the ummah, the international Muslim community, to be part of the world community of faiths, nations and peoples. The essence of the Koranic vision is the duty of believers to take the lead in forming new coalitions across all dividing lines to promote what is right, and prevent what is wrong.

Muslims have no monopoly on right, on what is good, on justice, or the intellectual and moral reflexes that promote these necessities. The Koran calls on Muslims to set aside all sectarianism and work with people of good conscience whoever they may be, wherever they are, to serve the needs of the neediest. This, for me, is the true jihad, the jihad that is crying out for the attention of Muslims everywhere.

Movement towards synthesis requires the interplay of another central Islamic concept, namely: ijtihad. Ijtihad means 'reasoned struggle for understanding', struggle to comprehend the contemporary meaning of Islamic precepts and principles. It is a cognate of jihad, one that expands the meaning of the term. Interpretation of the meaning of Islam is an act of culpable negligence by educated Muslims the world over. We have left the exposition of our faith in the hands of undereducated elites, religious scholars whose lack of comprehension of the contemporary world is usually matched only by their disdain and contempt for all its ideas and cultural products. Islam has been permitted to languish as the professional domain of people more familiar with the world of the eleventh century than the twenty-first century we now inhabit. And this class has buried ijtihad – a conventional source

of Islamic law and wisdom as well as the basic conceptual instrument for adjusting to change – into frozen
and distant history.

The betrayal of ijtihad has enabled obscurantism to
dominate the life of Muslim communities. It has lead
to the pernicious irreligion of the Taliban who deny
women the right to education and work in direct violation of the responsibilities laid upon women by the
Koran. They are akin to all those religious adepts who
complain that democracy and human rights are 'infidel
inventions' because their terminology and institutional
form are not shaped in the conceptual framework of
Islam. This is the unreason that has become the prime
obstacle to the reasoned struggle of one fifth of humanity to live in dignity, freedom, justice and peace.

The events of September 11 make it clear that ordinary
Muslims cannot be complacent about the interpretations
of their faith. We have to find a way to unleash the
best intentions, the essential values of Islam, from the
rhetoric of war, hatred and insularity that is as much
the stock in trade of mullahs as it is of unenlightened
policy advisers in the United States. That means all
educated and concerned Muslims must take responsibility for authoring twenty-first-century interpretations
of the basic concepts of Islam. From the ubiquitous and
reductive idea of jihad as Holy War we must move to
a more holistic notion of jihad for peace. From a reductive interpretation that limits ijma to an authoritarian
elite, we must develop contemporary, effective and
operable models for democratic and participatory
notions of consensus. Finally, we must revive ijtihad as

the dynamic principle for seeking a more humane understanding of our faith. In short, we have to go forward to the intrinsic meaning of Islam: peace.

Ziauddin Sardar

Society is Only as Strong as its Weakest Link

The events of the morning of September 11 stand out with a surreal, terrifying clarity. All too predictably real and human, however, has been the confused course of subsequent events. Despite assurances that the US military wasn't about to fire a $20 million rocket at a $10 tent, that is exactly what is happening. One early casualty of the terrorist attacks was supposed to be irony. But irony is thriving, when brutalized Afghan people, who have been denied adequate access to education or the media, find themselves suffering again for an unclear war aim. In that, they share something with the thousands of innocent Americans who died on September 11.

The mass suffering of innocents has always been part of what's often referred to as war's 'collateral damage'. Correct me if I'm wrong, but it seems that only during the last century have civilian populations become particular targets in times of conflict. In the new century even more so, and the military mentality that plans for a war between opposing armies, suitably equipped and defined, is irrelevant. Nothing made this more obvious than the American administration's obsession with a multi-billion dollar missile defence shield at the same time as a handful of knife-wielding fanatics were planning to bring the country to a standstill with not much more than $100,000 and a plan that was inconceivably audacious in its simplicity.

So the answers to the terrifying questions posed by September 11 clearly involve alternatives to the attitudes that prevailed prior to the attacks. I feel everyone is lost. An eye for an eye inevitably leads to blindness, but I know that as much as I deplore the military response we have seen to date, the apocalyptic nihilism we're confronted by isn't about to be placated by traditional diplomacy. Along with many people who normally share my anti-war sentiments, I accept that some kind of punitive action is necessary, but it can't be based on the 'give 'em hell Harry' approach that favours missiles over on-the-ground human intelligence.

It is also quite clear that the conflict between the Israelis and Palestinians must finally be settled: a challenge almost as enormous as the consequences if it is not resolved. After years of being content to play the easily distracted policeman of the world, America has woken up to the fact that it is also a citizen of that world. There are no longer conflicts that can be dismissed as local. In this respect, interconnectedness is potentially as much a weakness as a strength in the modern world.

But I prefer to focus on the area where I feel reassured that I can make a contribution. I am a born trader. Trade is one of the oldest and most honourable human endeavours. The ethical business movement seeks to preserve it as such, as something that protects and promotes human rights, justice and widening economic opportunity. September 11 and subsequent events have presented a challenge to our values. The values of freedom and fairness, not the prime motivators greed and exploitation, must become the transparent motivation for globalizing the world.

Prevalent global business practices have exacerbated crime, poverty, disease and social disparity. Such businesses are characterized by forced labour, sweatshops, child labour, the poisoning of air, water and land, the dislocation of entire communities, brutal dictatorships and gross inequalities of wealth. We like to think multinationals operate within the law. But what are their values? Do they include human rights and democracy? How do their global policies affect the rights of indigenous people and rural farmers? The perfect paradigm is the role of the oil multinationals, particularly in Burma, Nigeria and the Middle Eastern countries, places where the United States and the United Kingdom are now desperately trying to claim allies. Just look at how our representatives remain silent about human rights abuses in Saudi Arabia. At the very least, the silence makes the West morally inconsistent. The roots of hatred for Western policies are quite comprehensible when one experiences at grass-roots level the negative impact of globalization's stock in trade.

Organized crime, the drug trade, the black market in weapons, toxic waste and ozone depleting chemicals, the sex industries in Eastern Europe and the Orient, and sweatshop economies everywhere, are mobilizing worker armies of poorly monitored and dangerously neglected urban squatters, refugees and economic immigrants on behalf of the global shadow economy. Five or so years ago, Manuel Castells, a sociology professor at Berkeley, made some profound observations about the twentieth century being shaped by 'the excluded excluding the excluders', with non-partisan terrorism as their most likely weapon. The roots of future conflict are to be found not among these dispossessed and poor but within the current global policies that create them and will eventually provoke them into retaliation.

A society is only as strong as its weakest link. September 11 proved that even the Western world's strongholds become vulnerable when the weakest links in the world are ignored. I can't help but feel that there would be much less support for terrorists if their powerful targets were helping weak nations deal with debt, famine, Aids, the drug trade and all the detritus that the West has heaped on them over the decades. As one highly decorated retired general, who is opposed to the bombing, recently told the *Guardian*: 'Those who have food, security and prospects will not want to kill or be killed.'

So, how will this ideal situation be brought about?

I believe it is crucial to keep rural life vital and therefore abate the surge of millions into the squalor of overpopulated cities. Political stability and sustainable democracy can be helped by preventing conflict created by prevailing business practices. Every bit of pressure helps: campaigning for an end to arms; refusing to trade with despots and human rights abusers; finding an alternative to the major economic planning models; setting up small-scale, fair-trade initiatives or networking and sharing best practices with socially responsible businesses.

We need to recognize the rights and contributions of indigenous peoples who bring life-affirming leadership to the task of conserving the earth and its creatures. We need to understand that indigenous wisdom constitutes one of human society's most important and irreplaceable resources. We also need to embrace the fact that gender balance is essential to sustainable development: women's roles, needs, values and wisdom are especially central to decision-making for a new global reality. Women should be involved on an equal basis with men at all levels of policy-making, planning and implementation.

The global economic impact of women can be felt in the small-scale, grass-roots initiatives that women have been so instrumental in establishing in the majority of the world. Initiatives such as The Body Shop's Community Trade programme deal directly with economically marginalized communities and co-operatives around the globe. It is clear that economic opportunity means much more to women than money. It is empowering because it fosters the fundamentals of self-esteem: education, health care, cultural community and the chance to protect the past while shaping the future.

A sense of community is one of the so-called feminine values that ethical business thinkers actively promote. Such values reflect intimate personal and cultural attributes, which are in many ways the reverse of the global market syndrome, in its distance, impersonality and feckless capitalism. I have no doubt that feminized economic activity and economic relations are a desirable and workable way forward and that female financial pioneers will fundamentally change global economics.

We must shift from a private greed to a public good, for the sake of millions of lives. Issues such as the redistribution of wealth and economic globalization have moved up the political agenda, because a global community which doesn't address them is a dangerous place. However small-scale, initiatives which hold out the chance for economic independence can provide communities with the ability to guarantee their environment and their cultural identity – and, therefore, their future.

Ultimately, there is no other way to restore the sense of security and stability that the Western world lost in September 2001.

Anita Roddick

Pandora's Box

War on Terrorism

Since the atrocities on September 11 in America, more innocent people continue to die each day. Victims are being buried in New York, Washington and Pennsylvania and also in Tel Aviv, Kabul and Jalalabad. Pandora's Box has been opened and the violence is escalating unabated. The question is how can the lid be closed? Violence breeds violence and for all the grand rhetoric of Prime Minister Tony Blair a new world order is not waiting around the corner.

West versus East

The political leadership in Britain fails to truly understand the Muslim world, while President Bush struggles to find Islamic states on a world map. It is an indictment of the current and past foreign policies of Western countries that humanitarian gestures to developing nations in no way deliver global justice or eliminate poverty, disease and oppression.

The causes of terrorism are broad and deep. There is no excuse for killing, injuring or threatening individuals, but it is futile for a war to be declared on terrorism when you cannot fight and destroy the use of violent tactics designed to fulfil political ends.

It is first necessary to isolate the individuals by tackling the root causes. There will always be terrorists but they will not always enjoy popular support. Terrorists prey on oppressed people from whom they take succour. Remove the oppression through peaceful means and a key pillar of terrorism falls away. The answer to the brutal conflict in and around Israel is to create a new State of Palestine next to the State of Israel, sharing Jerusalem. Peace will only be achieved when the poison of tit-for-tat killing is ended and for that to happen the Israeli government has to recognize the Palestinian right to self-determination.

In the West most people, including government politicians and their advisers, fail to comprehend the Muslim world and faith. According to Gai Eaton, in *Islam and the Destiny of Man*, Muslims identify someone in terms of the religion into which they are born rather than in terms of their nationality. Even atheists and agnostics are still regarded as belonging in the Christian world.[1]

That is why support will grow when Muslims are being killed in Afghanistan and elsewhere while the sympathy for the United States may be waning. You cannot wipe out 1400 years of religious and political history and 100 years of US foreign policy with a few soundbites in the twenty-first century.

Economic Globalization

While Western children walk around in £100 trainers produced for a wage pittance by workers in poor countries, 30,000 children in developing nations die every day from preventable diseases.[2]

Although the British government has helped lead the campaign to reduce Third World debt, there is a long way to go to end the cycle of unsustainable repayments. Each day developing nations repay £40 million to the wealthy West; money that they simply cannot afford and which fails to dent the mountain of money they owe.[3]

With a higher incidence of natural disasters such as earthquakes, droughts, floods and cyclones, developing nations endlessly struggle to provide schools, hospitals, basic sanitation and clean water supplies.

The United States refusal to back the Kyoto Protocol, which in itself still does not adequately address the generally agreed increases in climate change, is symptomatic of their isolationist policies pre-September 11. This approach is underpinned by the hypocrisy of such battles as that at the World Trade Organization, where Bush's administration tried to stop Brazil and South Africa from trying to bypass pharmaceutical company patents to allow HIV/Aids drugs to be produced cheaply, to allow the treatment of the millions of infected victims in their continents. Yet now the United States blithely talks of ignoring the Cipro, anti-anthrax pill patent to allow mass production to counter the terrorist threat to their citizens.

A handful of rich countries come close to fulfilling their obligations to the United Nations by paying 0.7 per cent of their Gross Domestic Product to poor countries. After seven years of a Labour government barely half that target will be paid each year by Britain.

Dominant international institutions such as the World Trade Organization, International Monetary Fund and World Bank require radical reform to allow poor countries a fair opportunity to access much needed funds without the onerous and despised ties to the Structural Adjustment Programmes.

The Limitations of British Parliamentary Democracy

So how do we demonstrate that the secular and democratic world poses a challenge to the Islamic world? By arresting hundreds of Muslims and detaining them for questioning in dawn raids across Britain in the aftermath of the terrorist attacks? Through the Home Secretary launching a new 'anti-democracy' bill in Parliament? By deporting asylum seekers without appeal, while police powers to trawl through retained computer data on British citizens are explicitly promised and compulsory identification cards are discussed? Such measures will erode freedoms and increase powers to control the British people.

But at least the mother of all parliaments has voted for this war in Afghanistan? At least the elected representatives of the people have had their say and debated a motion setting out support for the government's actions? In fact, the House of Commons has had three emergency recalls and is still subjected each week to grand statements on international developments by the Prime Minister and his ministers. But, as Members of Parliament, we have been refused the right to vote on whether or not we want this war.

Is there a precedent for voting in Parliament for a war? Ironically the then Conservative administration allowed a vote on the Gulf War to endorse UN Security Resolution 678 and accepted a humanitarian amendment by the then Labour opposition.[4]

The Royal Prerogative dates back to 1688 and the Glorious Revolution. Then, the dictatorial powers of the monarch were given to the Prime Minister of the day. In its day it was radical stuff and 100 years later inspired an American constitution that enshrined inalienable rights to its new frontier citizens (excluding native Americans).

Now, over three centuries later, Britain staggers on with the same ailing and failing democracy. Parliament is a lame duck institution with no written constitution and the Royal Prerogative extends so widely that its parameters are unknown.[5]

In the first emergency debate following the recall of Parliament back from its ridiculously long summer recess on September 14, I urged caution on the Prime Minister. By the third recall I demanded Parliament be given the right to vote on the war. The suggestion was brushed aside and on a point of order I later again asked the Speaker for a vote. I was ruled out of order and the House of Commons' Honourable Members jeered and laughed at the temerity of the demand.[6]

The world teeters on the brink of a terrible war between West and East, the American president declares a 'crusade', hundreds die in bombing raids and 2.5 million Afghans are threatened with starvation this winter, while American and British serviceman risk their lives. And British MPs think this is funny.

A New British Written Constitution

It is time for a Constitutional Commission (note: not a Royal Commission) to draw up proposals for a written constitution. Parliamentary renewal should include fixed term parliaments and prime ministers, rights of Parliament to recall itself, to authorize a declaration of war or military action, to veto prime ministerial appointments, to strengthen the Select Committee system and to reform the 'whipping' system so that backbenchers are given genuine rights to speak and vote freely.

The partial reform of the House of Lords is welcomed but it needs to be replaced with the introduction of a democratically elected Senate. The detested dictatorial powers of the Royal Prerogative should be consigned to history and a new Bill of Rights and improved freedom of information would give new enforceable rights to British citizens.[7]

A written constitution would provide the structural framework in Parliament for reinvigorating our democracy. But by itself it will not persuade people that they should take an active part in politics. In the 2001 general election barely half the voters in Britain bothered to vote for their next government. Two-thirds do not vote in local elections and over three-quarters did not see the point of voting in the 1999 European elections. It is clear the present democratic systems have failed.

Politics and politicians need to become relevant to local people in British communities. Only then will the nation truly feel empowered to make changes in conjunction with its government. That it takes less time to set up an e-mail account than for MPs to queue through the lobbies, casting a single vote in an archaic voting method, suggests that we must implement radical changes to procedural protocol in the Commons.

Referendums on key issues and public petitioning that forces parliamentary debates would help to deliver a modern democracy for the twenty-first century. But MPs should also be more accountable to their constituents, with minimum standards laid down for their performance. Annual reports on MPs' work should be published so that by demonstrating their accountability, MPs might begin to reconnect with disaffected citizens.

A Strong, Ethical United Nations

The implications of renewing Britain's democracy (and other democracies faced with similar disillusioned voters) must be extended to the international community. There has to be a reaffirmation of commitment to the one organization responsible for international peace and security. The United Nations was born in 1942. Three years later at the San Francisco conference it adopted its Charter. Apart from several amendments this has remained the bedrock of hope for a peaceful world.[8]

While nation states pay lip-service to the United Nations, rich nations ride roughshod over the spirit and text of the Charter. Henry Kissinger has said that realpolitik must be given a clear priority over the idealism of striving to conquer global evils.[9]

There is a glimmer of hope that with reform and the advent of a global economy and increasing trade, the West will see the need to reaffirm the importance of the United Nations, not least in order to protect and enhance its economies. But so far the war in Afghanistan shows that old habits die hard. UN Security Council Resolutions passed in the weeks after the terrorist attacks expressed sympathy for the US victims, confirmed the right to self-defence and declared that all necessary steps should be taken to counter the terrorism. At no point do those texts make mention of authorizing military action in Afghanistan or anywhere else.[10]

There is no UN mandate for the bombing or landing of troops inside the desperate country where one in four, including 300,000 children, starve each year. This winter an additional 100,000 children could die because the bombing is preventing food from getting through to them. An Oxfam worker has said 'We all know we don't have enough food for the winter [in Afghanistan]. Some people know that if this situation continues they will not survive.'[11]

The vague words and bullying of other states have

given carte blanche to the West (i.e. the United States and Great Britain) to do as they see fit. Although Australia, Belgium and France promise military support there is no promise of any Islamic states forming a military coalition.

Is there an alternative to the present action? I think so. There needs to be an emergency meeting of the UN General Assembly to agree the principle of military action to bring the culprits for the terror attacks on the United States to justice and to authorize the creation of an international criminal tribunal to give legal basis to this action.

International Criminal Tribunal

The British Foreign Secretary in the House of Commons on October 8 poured scorn on the idea of an international court to hear the evidence and indict those responsible for the American atrocities. He cited the example of the Lockerbie aeroplane bombing under the jurisdiction of a Scottish court (albeit held in The Netherlands) as the excuse not to invoke an international court. He explained that such a court could be set up after military action. However, earlier that day the Prime Minister had said that it was 'not a very serious consideration' to have to worry about indicting those alleged to be responsible.[12]

It is clear that the prime suspect will be executed through military action and a 'fair' trial is not an option. But even if it was, the suggestion that a US court should try those responsible shows the naive thinking in the

West. With a highly charged situation, how would Muslims react to an American judge and jury sitting and passing judgement? An international criminal tribunal in the absence of a permanent court (which the United States continues to block) is the credible way forward.[13] Such tribunals based upon UN Security Council Resolutions are successfully working to prosecute the criminals in the former Yugoslavia and Rwanda. One thousand two hundred staff work systematically and fairly to indict those responsible for their murderous deeds and bring them to justice.[14]

A proper mandate set out in arrest warrants would allow the international community to see the transparency and strictly judicial basis to the subsequent action. The US and British governments have refused to allow an international criminal tribunal to be set up and the only 'evidence' they produced was a document with some partial facts. That evidence was prefixed with: 'This document does not purport to provide a prosecutable case against Osama bin Laden in a court of law.'

Is it not a terrifying day for democracy when politicians arbitrarily decide someone's guilt and issue an execution order?

United Nations Security Council

As the international criminal tribunal meets, the UN Security Council should agree a new resolution to authorize specific military action under Article 43 of the UN Charter. This does not authorize unilateral or even multilateral action but lays down in precise terms how the Security Council can take control of any agreed military actions. With the assistance of a Military Staff Committee (Articles 46–8), consisting of chief staffs of the Permanent Members of the Security Council, the United Nations on behalf of the international community would decide the nature and limit of actions to be taken.

Special forces may have to be used to enforce the UN arrest warrants, but they would have an international legality and it is likely that bombing would be declared illegal.

Conclusion

East and West, peoples of all ethnicities, faiths, cultures and beliefs should aspire to a state of mutual respect and understanding. For this to occur, international law must be upheld and enforced through the United Nations.

Radical reform is long overdue to redistribute the wealth of the rich and invest in saving lives and building the infrastructure for the future. A new commitment by the West to the United Nations is needed to turn fine words into courageous actions in order to help developing nations eliminate hunger, disease and deprivation. Only then can terrorism be prevented and international peace achieved.

Paul Marsden
Member of Parliament for
Shrewsbury & Atcham

SOURCES

1 *Islam and the Destiny of Man*, by Gai Eaton
2 UNICEF report, 1998
3 'HIPC – flogging a dead process', report by Jubilee Plus, 2001
4 Hansard, debate, 21 January 1991, Column 113
5 Hansard, Prime Minister written reply, 16 October 2001
6 Hansard, debate, 8 October 2001, Column 829
7 *A Written Constitution for the United Kingdom*, by IPPR, 1993
8 United Nations Charter, 1945 (amended 1965, 1968)
9 *Diplomacy*, by Henry Kissinger, 1994
10 UN Security Resolutions 1363 and 1373
11 'The humanitarian situation in Afghanistan and on its borders', by Oxfam International
12 Hansard, debate, 8 October 2001, Column 820
13 *Adapting the UN to a Postmodern Era*, ed. W. Andy Knight, 2001, p. 99
14 The International Criminal Court Bill, House of Commons Library paper 01/39, 2001

Make Law, Not War

On an international level, making law is much harder than making war. The immediate and rightful response to the atrocity of September 11 was to demand 'justice', but that word sounded, in some powerful mouths, like the cry of the lynch mob for summary execution, assassination squads and the prime suspect's head on a plate. If any silver lining is ever to be found in those grotesque pictures of the black cloud over New York City, it can only come from a commitment to a system of global justice which alone offers a principled method of punishing what truly amounts to a crime against humanity.

The confusion over what 'justice' requires became acute when America chose 'Operation Infinite Justice' as its first brand name for the bombing of Afghanistan. It made no philosophical sense, because human justice is both finite and fallible. More importantly, it begged the question – which Western leaders have so notably failed to address – of exactly what procedure they proposed to adopt to persuade the rest of the world that their cause is right. NATO's attack on Serbia was justified in order to stop ethnic cleansing in Kosovo: Milosevic on trial was an early war aim that has now come to pass. The economic war on Libya found its objective, and its resolution, in the Lockerbie Tribunal. This war on terrorism can only be 'won' by putting in place an effective – and, necessarily, a fair – system for punishing the authors of atrocities and hence deterring those minded to perpetrate them in the future.

International Law, it must at once be acknowledged, justifies breaching 'state sovereignty' – the refuge of scoundrels like Pinochet and Milosevic – when force is necessary in self-defence or to punish a crime against humanity. The International Court of Justice declared in 1949, in a ruling sought by Britain when its ships in the Corfu Channel were attacked from Albania, that every state has a duty to prevent its territory being used for unlawful attacks on other states. In 1980, after the hostage taking at the US Embassy, the same court ruled that Iran was responsible for a failure in 'vigilance' and a toleration of terrorism. It follows that the right of self-defence (preserved in Article 51 of the UN Charter) permits the United States to resort to force for the limited purpose of doing Afghanistan's duty, after that state refused to extradite Osama bin Laden and to close down his camps.

But America's legal right of self-defence does not stretch to overthrowing a government or embarking on an indefinite bombing campaign. The precedent which places the severest legal limit on the US attack was established by its own protest against Britain's sinking in 1837 of a US steamboat (the *Caroline*) which was aiding rebels in Canada: both governments agreed that self-defence must be based on a necessity which is 'instant, overwhelming, leaving no choice of means, and no moment for deliberation'. Self-defence is a blunt and somewhat primitive doctrine, which leaves too much scope to the subjective assessment of a self-defender bent on revenge.

A more modern, and more sophisticated, legal justification for an armed response is provided by the emerging human rights rule that requires international action to prevent and to punish 'crimes against humanity'. The September 11 atrocities, like the bombings of the US embassies in Kenya and Tanzania in 1998, precisely fit the definition, which covers not only genocide and torture but 'multiple acts of murder committed as part of a systematic attack against a civilian population'. It was to punish such crimes in Kosovo that NATO breached Serbian sovereignty, and the same principles should apply (and this time, there is Security Council backing) to the attack in Afghanistan.

But this means, importantly for the present conflict, that the attack on Afghanistan must have a legitimate objective, defined in terms of the justification for the incursion. If, as President Bush insists, that objective is justice, there must be produced not only presumptive evidence of guilt but also a fair procedure for bringing the suspects to trial.

I have anxiously considered the case against Osama bin Laden and the Taliban leadership tabled in the UK Parliament in October 2001. It is not 'evidence' so much as argument based on similar facts, matters of record, and intelligence analysis: even so, it shows in blood-curdling detail that Osama bin Laden has consistently incited the murder of Americans and has confessed to involvement in the 1998 US embassy bombings in East Africa. To dismiss the case against his organization for responsibility over September 11 as 'circumstantial' is to miss the point: in proving conspiracy, as every criminal lawyer knows, circumstantial evidence is often more credible than fallible human testimony. It amounts at the very least to a *prima facie* case of mass murder for racist motives, and it has become more compelling since. Osama bin Laden stands accused not merely as a peripatetic gang leader, but as a state actor: a crucial ally and agent of the Government of Afghanistan. The Taliban leadership stands similarly accused, of aiding and abetting his preparations for a genocidal jihad against Americans (and anyone else who happens to get in the way).

These charges are as grave, and as well-substantiated, as those against Karadic and Mladic over Srebrenica (where seven thousand Muslim men and boys were exterminated), and against Milosevic and his political and military leadership for the ethnic cleansing of Muslims in Kosovo. What is common to all these crimes is that they are 'against humanity' precisely because the fact that fellow humans can conceive and commit these diminishes us all. As defined by the 1998 Rome Treaty for an international criminal court, a 'crime against humanity' includes a systematic attack deliberately directed against a civilian population involving acts of multiple murder. The evidence against Osama bin Laden and the Taliban leadership for involvement in such a crime committed on September 11 demands to be answered at a trial. Whether, when it is fleshed out and forensically tested, it would create a certainty of guilt must be a matter for a court. But which court? Milosevic is on trial in The Hague, and Karadic and Mladic (NATO willing) cannot be far behind. But what court awaits the Taliban and Osama bin Laden?

It is at this point that an embarrassed silence descends on the war leadership. For all the talk of 'justice', the preferred option appears to be a cold-blooded killing of Osama bin Laden and a mere removal of the Taliban leadership, supplanted either by a US-imposed puppet government or (more likely) a UN protectorate. The only 'trial' conceivably on offer is before a jury empanelled in New York. The plain fact is that a jury trial in New York, with a death sentence upon conviction, will not provide a forum where justice can be seen to be done.

A New York jury will be too emotionally involved in the events to consider the evidence dispassionately. (For this reason, those accused of IRA crimes in Britain were never tried in the cities they were alleged to have bombed.) It may be doubted whether any American jury could put aside the prejudice against the 'prime suspect' created by their media and by their leader's demands for his 'head on a plate'. The spectacle which would follow – a death sentence by lethal injection – is too grotesque to contemplate. The only 'guilty' verdict which can persuade the world of Osama bin Laden's guilt will not be delivered in one word from 'twelve angry men', but will be closely and carefully reasoned, delivered by distinguished jurists, some from

Muslim countries, at an international criminal court.

There is just such a court in the planning stages, building upon the precedents set by The Hague tribunal in its 'ad hoc' jurisdiction over state actors accused of crimes against humanity in ex-Yugoslavia and Rwanda. Its statute, approved by 120 nations in Rome in 1998, affords all basic rights to defendants, in trials before three international judges and appeals to a further five. It has protocols for evaluating the kind of hearsay evidence which may be necessary to prove terrorist conspiracies, and which protect the recording of electronic intercepts and other fruits of secret intelligence gathering. It was, in fact, first suggested (by Mikhail Gorbachev) as a means of punishing international terrorists. Its statute has so far been ratified by forty-two nations (including Britain, France and Russia). It will come into existence when sixty nations ratify – on present indications, by the end of 2002.

The obvious opportunity created by the coalition against terrorism forged after September 11, supported by all permanent members of the Security Council, was to bring the International Criminal Court (ICC) into being immediately, with a retrospective mandate to investigate, try and punish the perpetrators and abettors of terrorist actions against the US. The problem, ironically, is that the most formidable opponent of the ICC has been the Pentagon, allied with the Jesse Helms faction of the Republican party, obsessed with the notion that US sovereignty would be degraded if an American were ever indicted as a war criminal. Their latest wheeze has been to promote in Congress the misnamed 'American Servicemembers Protection Act', designed to sabotage the court by withdrawing US co-operation and even permitting the President to use force to free any American ever 'captured' by The Hague Tribunal. One would have hoped that the message of September 11 – that we need much more, not less, inter-national co-operation to ensure that perpetrators have no place to hide – would have led to the abandonment of the irresponsible initiative. Yet only a fortnight later – on 25 September 2001 – George W. Bush gave this 'bomb The Hague' bill his support.

This self-indulgent isolationism demonstrates how remote the Bush administration still is from giving any real support to international criminal justice. We owe that very idea to President Truman, who insisted on the Nuremberg trials against the opposition of Churchill (who wanted the Nazi leaders shot on sight). He did so because 'undiscriminating executions or punishments without definite findings of guilt, fairly arrived at, would not sit easily on the American conscience or be remembered by our children with pride'.

Perhaps it needs Mr Blair to remind the President of how 'the American conscience' once cooled the British desire for revenge and created a court at Nuremberg whose judgement stands as a landmark in civilization's fight against racially-motivated terror. Its legacy requires the arrest of Osama bin Laden for the crimes of 1998 as much as 2001 – and of his aiders and abettors, the Taliban mullahs who so misused the state power they arrogated to themselves. But the force that is designed to achieve it, through the bombing of Afghanistan and the collateral killing and maiming of innocent civilians, can only be justified if the overall objective is to put on a fair trial the men accused of crimes against humanity. Unless and until this becomes a war aim, stated and stuck to irrespective of any opportunity for summary execution, the war will have as much to do with 'justice' as the Red Queen's cry in *Alice's Adventures in Wonderland*: 'Sentence first – trial later.'

Geoffrey Robertson

The Presence of Justice

We all long for peace. But peace can be a deceptive and dangerous word. When Hitler invaded Czechoslovakia all he asked was to be left in peace. When terrorists hide away, again, all they ask is to be left in peace. When Martin Luther King was in prison because of his work for civil rights, a group of white pastors wrote to tell him to stop disturbing the peace. He wrote back to say: 'Peace is not the absence of tension but the presence of justice.' Certainly, in the Bible, peace is always inseparable from justice. The great Hebrew word shalom means a just and ordered peace in which every human being is able to flourish.

On this earth, peace and justice will often be in tension. In order to establish a true peace, based on justice, it will sometimes be necessary to disturb the apparent, false peace. But when justice is being sought by the use of arms, as it is at the present moment, two attitudes in particular need to be avoided. First, the idea that right is all on one side. This can lead to a crusade mentality with the idea, in religious terms, that it is a fight on God's side against God's enemies. There is an inevitable ambiguity about all human decision-making that precludes any self-righteousness.

The second approach to be avoided at a time like

this is a refusal to contemplate the difficult, dangerous decisions that have to be made whether we like it or not. All sides to the conflict are flawed, for we live in a fallen world. But there is no moral equivalent between that fragile human achievement which we know as civilization and the terrorism that seeks to destroy it. Our choices have to be made with all the consequences of them realistically considered. As the great theologian and political thinker Reinhold Niebuhr wrote in 1940:

> There is nothing in our Christian faith which allows us to escape the monumental decisions and destinies of history. We must contend against evil, even though we know that we are ourselves involved in the evil against which we contend. We must seek to do the will of God and yet not forget that in his sight no man (not one) living is justified. We must work for the greatest possible justice in human society and yet know that sinful self-interest will corrupt every scheme of justice that we elaborate.

In the world as we have it, it is not possible to contain terrorism without the use of armed force: nevertheless force is only part of the equation. Studies of guerrilla movements and terrorist groups since World War II have shown that their primary objective has always been a political one. They have never been able to win great military victories. Their strategy has been to create enough disturbance and stay in existence long enough until their constituency is widened and their political goal achieved. If this is the nature of terrorism, then counter-terrorist measures need to have the same perspective. In short, the crucial factor is the constituency to which the terrorists are trying to appeal. Whether or not they succeed will depend upon the degree of alienation of that constituency and the extent to which they are able to motivate and mobilize it in their support. Our political leaders well understand this, of course, which is why the United States, together with the crucial support of the United Kingdom, went to so much trouble to build up an alliance and why they will continue to see holding the alliance together as a continuing priority. Governments in many Islamic countries are precarious. It has been said to me by a leading Muslim historian that not a single Islamic government has the support of its people in the current struggle against the al-Qaeda network. Whether or not this is true those governments are certainly caught between appeals from the West and many members of their own population who are strongly anti-American.

If the issue in the world today is primarily political and only secondarily military, then it is the relationship between the Islamic world and the West that really matters. Here, I believe, the Christian churches have a crucial role to play, and in many places they are playing it. In many towns in the United Kingdom, for example, Christian and Muslim communities have been building good relationships.

In 1938, when the Munich Agreement was signed, T. S. Eliot wrote that he experienced a sense of moral shock. It seemed that those opposed to Nazism had nothing better to defend than a cluster of banks and insurance companies and believed in nothing more substantial than a good rate of interest on dividends. The Muslim world also has such criticisms of the West. Leaving aside objections to American foreign policy, which are, of course, very serious and fundamental, there is a widespread sense of distaste at the West's vulgar consumerism. In response to Munich, T. S. Eliot wrote his famous essay on the idea of a Christian society. But what he put forward there could in fact well describe a civilized society. He defined it as one 'in which the natural end of man – virtue and wellbeing in community – is acknowledged for all, and the supernatural end – beatitude – for those who have the eyes to see it'. Over the centuries Islam has also been associated with great civilizations; based at Damascus, Baghdad, Cairo and Constantinople: civilizations from which the West has learnt a lot. It is not necessary to believe with Samuel Huntington that there is an inevitable 'clash of civilizations'. For Christians, Muslims and, indeed, secularists I think can unite around T. S. Eliot's definition. Terrorism seeks to destroy civilization whether it is Christian, Muslim or secular. Christians, Muslims and secularists need to unite in defending civilization against all that threatens it. Alas, we still have a very long way to go before any agreement can be reached about how, now, we can best protect and build up such a civilization. But there could, I believe, be substantial agreement about the nature of civilization and the values which are necessary to sustain it.

The Rt Revd Richard Harries
Bishop of Oxford

The Devil's Complaint

There is an eastern tale about a man who goes to complain to the Devil. Deeply troubled by the suffering he observes in the world, he asks the Devil how it is that he is able to cause so much evil, so much pain, so much chaos.

'I am innocent,' protests the Devil, 'of all these accusations. I am blamed for everything, but I hardly do anything.'

'Explain,' says the man.

'I'll show you,' says the Devil.

Nearby, the Devil finds a large ram, tethered to a stake in the ground. 'Now watch carefully,' says the Devil. 'All I am going to do is loosen the stake slightly – that's all.'

And the Devil loosens the stake.

The ram tosses its head and pulls the stake free. Seeing the open door of its master's house, it wanders inside. By the entrance is a large mirror, and taking the reflection for another ram, the ram charges into it, shattering the mirror into fragments. The owner's wife, running downstairs and seeing her precious family heirloom destroyed, cries to her servants: 'Kill that ram!'

Now the ram had been a special pet of the husband, who returns home and finds his beloved pet has been killed on his wife's order. He is enraged, but his wife shows no remorse.

'I divorce you,' he tells his wife.

The wife moves in with her relatives, who feel she has been unfairly treated, and a delegation is sent to the husband to complain. The husband dismisses them, and protects his home with armed guards. In turn, the opposing relatives arm themselves, and the conflict escalates. Rival houses are burned down, a local man is killed, and a feud ensues, spreading to neighbouring villages. Soon the entire area has divided into warring camps as the casualties mount. The conflict spreads . . .

The Devil turns to the man and says: 'See? How can you blame me for all these terrible things? All I did was loosen a stake!'

The stake has been loosened. War has been declared. Our species has proved itself once again incapable of circumventing the deliberate destruction of human life, and its righteous, sometimes passionate pursuit.

At the same time, people all over the planet – perhaps more people than ever – are asking questions about war: its origins, its results and its possible remedies. Nothing is new in these questions, nor in their likely answers. Just as war has been waged in almost every era, so too have questions regarding validity and alternative strategies for resolving conflict.

I think it is timely to remind ourselves of what is

already known. We know that, under ordinary conditions, war is universally repugnant. We know, generally, that wars cause more problems than they solve. We know of the brutality and injustices that occur during war, of the social and economic disruption which it causes, and of the wholly tragic suffering of the innocent whose lives are shattered by war.

We know, in times when our blood is cooler, about the contagious reductionism by which the 'enemy' becomes a faceless 'evildoer' for whom no punishment is too harsh; about the mass susceptibility of nations to the rhetoric that surrounds war; about the awesome process by which communities, nations and entire continents are swept up in the contagion of conflict.

We know too, as we are made increasingly aware of how small our planet really is, that the fundamental wishes and goals of human beings are not so terribly different in lands and cultures other than our own; to live, in short, and live meaningfully.

And we know even that many people enjoy war – this, perhaps more than any other, is an aspect of human behaviour we are keenest to forget.

How is it that, periodically and in virtually every generation, we remain susceptible to the persuasion that the destruction of human life, together with all of its consequences, is not only desirable but wholly justifiable? And stranger yet, perhaps, that we look back on the more brutal chapters of history with both regret and incredulity, asking ourselves how such things could have happened.

It is the hardest thing to face this question honestly,

and to study it without shrinking from the results. It would be presumptuous to posit an answer; but I believe that, more than ever, it has become our individual responsibility to address this question; no institution can do the job for us. War is a human affliction; it concerns all of humanity. History teaches us that all peoples in every era are susceptible to the pathology of war, and no group or creed should put itself above the need to ask the question. But to be satisfied with an answer in terms of economics, nationality or ideology is insufficient; the problem lies further back, somewhere deeper in human nature.

I believe that an understanding of war – and correspondingly, of peace – must be searched for, observed and pondered in our own individual experience. To do so requires the willingness to examine our own private attitudes and secret prejudices, our convictions and beliefs, our grievances, our susceptibility to powerful emotions (which we may find are not, in the end, our own) – all these and a thousand other very human habits that in ordinary life go largely unquestioned. For the most sincere, to do so will mean meeting face to face not only with human primitivism but, more frighteningly, that prodigious human skill in rationalizing its own most monstrous attributes.

No surprise, perhaps, that humanity has proved a reluctant candidate for the challenge.

But only by meeting it can knowledge – which we do not lack – become understanding, of which we are in dire need – and from which meaningful change in the world itself can spring.

*   *   *

Dare I suggest that some good may be hidden in the present dangers? I do not think it is too much to suggest that we are at some kind of threshold in our potential evolution or at least an opportunity of enormous significance. Suddenly an unprecedented dialogue is taking place around the globe; people are exchanging ideas and concerns across continents.

This is because war has been brought, as it were, to our doorsteps; no longer can countries that formerly felt themselves invulnerable remain so; no longer can they wage war against a distant enemy and remain utterly untouched by the consequences. At no time has the connectedness of the world been felt more keenly. This is good, because we are faced with the necessary challenge of thinking in new ways closer to us all. How are we to protect our livelihoods, if we cannot fence out – or defeat outright – our enemies? Who, indeed – and what – are our true enemies?

And in seeking more creative ways to deliver ourselves from danger, we may discover what those who advocate war are likely to dread: that warfare is an outdated means by which to ensure our common human interests. We may also be led to the conviction that nothing less than a complete overhaul of humanity's ideas about itself is required, and that there is no better time to undertake the task than now.

I believe that an increasing portion of humanity is willing to rise to this challenge. I am personally heartened by the number of people who are shocked at the futility of the present violence; who have no confidence in a military solution, who are convinced of the necessity of re-evaluating our traditionally accepted ideas about solving conflict through conflict, and who are not distracted by issues of politics, doctrine or creed.

Peace is not a utopian dream. It is a universal exigency. But so long as this remains only a concept, rather than a practice, it is wishful thinking.

If we accept the axiom that war is infinitely less desirable than peace – I mean really accept it, and not be derailed by the usual rationalizations for destroying life – we will understand that peace is not only more urgent than ever, but also that its realization can only begin in the individual: the conflicts in human affairs are the mirror of the conflicts in the individual. But so too are their resolutions. Why should peace, instead of war, not be our legacy to our descendants? What holds us back? If societies are prepared to accept the necessity of a long military campaign – why not a long peaceful campaign?

Peace – personal peace, national peace, global peace – is, I believe, largely realizable: it begins here and now, with a choice. For if war is a uniquely human trait, so too is the ability to make choices. At the opposite end of the scale from human barbarity lies human wisdom, which arises from a choice: the choice to observe itself as a species, to step back coolly from itself, to separate, as it were, from itself – and from this wisdom, to learn and grow. Difficult as it is I believe this choice is open to all.

Jason Elliot

A River Runs Through It

In the Jordan Valley, not far from Jericho, on the Israeli-occupied West Bank, a river runs down from the hills.

It's called the Ein Al-Auja – Auja's stream: it shares its name with the village whose fields it watered for generations.

When I (Martin) went there, many years ago, Auja's citrus trees were being abandoned, and many villagers were leaving, too. The stream that had fed their fields had run dry. The reason lay a few miles west, at the end of an uphill track, at the source where the water tumbled out from the hills. The stream head was walled round and guarded by a couple of soldiers. From the nearby slopes, you could see how its flow had been diverted away from its namesake Arab village, and into what were now the lush fields of a new Israeli settlement. A little blue pearl of a swimming pool sparkled among the new buildings.

Some weeks later, I saw a photo of this settlement, or one very much like it, its bright green patchwork an apparent miracle in a dry land. It featured in a tourist leaflet celebrating how Israeli ingenuity had 'made the desert bloom'.

I remember wondering whether they'd rename the stream . . . And thinking how bitterly ironic it is, that it's not the supposedly irreconcilable differences between people which pitch them into war, but the things we most have in common – our need for sweet water, good land, and a home . . .

It is of course a mug's game, even at the best of times, to mix realpolitik and the moral high ground. And these are certainly not the best of times. But it's simply impossible *not* to make the connection between our vision of a more compassionate, more equitable, sustainable world – and the events of September 11, and their Afghan aftermath.

At the most basic level, we don't have to look much beyond the Middle East to see how a failure to turn that vision into anything approaching reality can breed conflict. You don't need a degree in environmental management to spot that the refugee camps of the Gaza Strip, for example, are an object lesson in unsustainability – and as such, a perfect seedbed for fanaticism.

This is not for one moment to cast the group of callous murderers who killed thousands in Manhattan as some rather overenthusiastic form of eco-warrior. But the support which men such as Osama bin Laden attract among the poor and the dispossessed is undoubtedly fed by that combination of social injustice and environmental degradation which is the very definition of unsustainable development. In Maoist terms, it's those people who provide the sea of sympathy in which the fish of al-Qaeda swim. And you can't drain that sea by force of arms. Military might can kill individual terrorists (a word strangely reserved almost exclusively for those who attack Westerners): it rarely saps their support. For proof, look at Palestine, where decades of Israeli *force majeure* have only fed successive *intifadas*.

Draining that sea of sympathy must surely include addressing the root causes of injustice and degradation with a resolve which we've sadly lacked to date. At ground level, action programmes on sustainable development can be a crucial part of breaking the vicious circle of poverty, alienation and despair which feeds fanaticism.

We should not, of course, be lured into making too many glib connections here: sympathy for the terrorists' agenda may be strongest in some of the world's poorest countries, but there is no simple link between poverty and terrorism – or indeed, between globalization and poverty. Though this is fiercely contested terrain, most development economists see a positive relationship between international trade and economic growth, reducing rather than increasing absolute poverty. Some have even argued that the reason Afghanistan is so poor is not globalization, but the lack of it.

That said, we in the West haven't properly internalized what it means to live in a global economy. Though its fruits may not be equitably distributed, the hype about its supposed benefits surely is. Once Afghanistan is 'liberated' from the isolationist zealotry of the Taliban, even its remotest villages will over time be exposed to a media onslaught extolling the glories of Western consumerism. For the vast majority, though, the gulf between daily reality and the riches displayed in that onslaught is unimaginably huge. They can all too easily seem no more than a distant dream jealously guarded by the military and financial muscle of America and its allies. So should we really be surprised if the world's 2 billion people surviving on less than $2 a day end up responding with a mix of anger, envy, and intense bitterness? Or that some adopt ideologies that wholly reject Western values, and, *in extremis*, end up as conscripts in the extremists' jihad.

So where does this leave the 'war on terror'?

Well for starters, the much-vaunted talk of a war to safeguard 'democratic values' will mean diddly squat to those who presently have no vote or voice in the new world order, no security of food nor work, no hope of the kind of prosperity which we all but claim as a right, and who rarely register on the G8's radar unless they're dying – or killing – on a CNN scale . . .

Nor are they likely to be impressed by an assertion that we're waging war to protect 'our economy and way of life' – which can all too easily sound as though we're fighting for the freedom to go shopping: for every one of us to own a 4x4 without fear of assault. And which has, it must be said, to be set against the inescapable fact that the apogee of the American way of life á la Bush is deeply unsustainable: the reckless consumption of a hefty chunk of the world's common resources by a relatively small proportion of its people is most emphatically not a cause worth killing for. If this is a battle for 'business as usual', then it can only be a bitterly pyrrhic victory.

What's urgently needed now is for America, and Britain, to articulate a post-war vision which will speak to those far beyond their borders. To their credit, both President Bush and, in particular, Tony Blair in his speech to the Labour conference, have hinted at such a vision – but they could do so much more. They could uncover, and demonstrate, a mixture of compassion and humility which has hardly been the West's forte, but which is a damn fine starting place for any sustained effort to make the world a more sustainable, and hence secure, home. It means a less frenzied promotion of interconnectedness, and a more conciliatory acknowledgement of *interdependence*. One which must, incidentally, be buttressed through strengthened global institutions and agreements. Bush's first few months of US-first unilateralism (during which he abrogated no less than six international treaties) sent out a disastrous message that the rest of the world counted for nothing to the most powerful nation on earth.

We isolate our thinking at our peril, because, as September 11 so viciously demonstrated, we cannot isolate ourselves. No missile defence shield could have halted the terrorists, nor saved the United States from biological attack. And for all we know, the next generation are not being trained in remote camps in Afghanistan, but in the computer departments of American universities. E-terrorism looms large as the next frontier – a frontier quite literally beyond all borders.

So aren't Bush and Blair right to assert that 'terrorism

now poses the greatest single threat to global security'? No: that simply reveals profound ignorance as to what is really undermining it.

This was borne in upon me (Jonathon), very uncomfortably, just a day after the New York and Washington attacks, when a close friend asked why I was more wound up about the 5000 who lost their lives than I was about the 40,000 or so who will have died somewhere in the world on September 11 as a result of preventable or easily treatable diseases. And, according to UNICEF, 50 per cent of those would have been children under the age of five.

The fact that we've all learned to live so easily with such a devastating, daily death-toll speaks volumes. It's morally impossible to argue that the value of one life in Bangladesh or Bolivia is worth less than one in New York or Washington.

This is not for a second to suggest that any course of action that doesn't include bringing justice to those responsible for the murders of September 11 is remotely appropriate. But unless it's pursued in a way which transparently addresses the basic injustices which feed fanaticism – and there is, to be frank, precious little sign of that as we write – then it's only pouring more fertilizer onto those seedbeds of violence. And condemning a lot more people to the repetitive brutalities endured by those who fail to learn from history. It's the strongest case, yet, perhaps, for being tough on crime, tough on its causes.

In this light, reducing our ecological footprint is not some feel-good gesture; it's one of the most persuasive tools of international diplomacy. Applying basic standards of social justice to decisions over international business is not a fad for fans of fair trade: it's our best insurance policy against fanaticism.

Almost without exception, technologies which are environmentally more sustainable are less prone to being hijacked, in any sense of the word, by those intent on harm. No terrorist is going to make governments tremble by threatening to bomb a wind turbine, or release clouds of compost over our cities. Compare that to the destructive potential of nuclear power and toxic chemicals. A more sustainable world is indeed a safer one.

More specifically, this is certain to focus American attention on the vulnerabilities of its addiction to oil. Despite enthusiastic development of its own reserves in Alaska and elsewhere, the United States can never hope to replace its desperate dependence on oil from the Middle East – not while it is so wedded to a carbon economy. That dependence, of course, is the prime reason for the presence of US troops in Saudi Arabia – a presence which, ironically, is one of the chief complaints of Osama bin Laden.

America would love to be self-sufficient in energy; it's just possible that, post-September, it will wake up to the realization that this means a decisive shift away from fossil fuels, towards the combination of renewables and efficiency gains to which it is surprisingly well suited. Against such a backdrop, its reservations about Kyoto would soon, of course, evaporate. And a move in this direction from the world's most powerful economy would surely drive a revolutionary pace of change elsewhere.

There must be a slim hope that the fear of terrorism will, paradoxically, focus attention on the absolute imperative that people with wildly divergent views learn how to talk to each other. One of the surprising triumphs of the sustainable development community is its remarkable progress in developing understanding between people of implacably opposed opinions. There was a time when it would have been inconceivable for industry to sit down with activists: to all intents and purposes, they came from different planets. Yet recent years have seen quite dramatic – and often wholly unsung – breakthroughs in this area, not only between business and campaigners, but within and among communities, too. There's even a village in Israel where Jews and Palestinians have succeeded in living alongside each other precisely as a result of such dialogue.

The trick, it seems, is to start with what we have in common, rather than with the opinions – even the religions – which divide us. And what we have in common are, quite simply, the resources on which all human life depends. We have to find a way to share those equitably, or we will surely go to war over them.

We've said before that it's easy to regard the pursuit of sustainability as a luxury of the good times – something appropriately eclipsed by the hard stuff of human conflict. But surely, now more than ever, the truth is that it's a fundamental prerequisite for that most desperately elusive of shared human desires – peace.

Voices for Peace

These days we seem to hear a lot about stark choices: about being either 'with us, or against us'. So here's another one, courtesy of Martin Luther King, which might just be a little more poignant for the years ahead: 'We learn to live together as brothers – or we die together as fools.'

Martin Wright and Jonathon Porritt

Contributor's Notes

KAREN ARMSTRONG

Writer and broadcaster Karen Armstrong is the winner of the Calmus Foundation Annual Award and the Muslim Public Affairs Council Media Award. Her television credits include *The First Christian*, *Tongues of Fire* and she is the author of several books including *Through the Narrow Gate*, *The Gospel According to Woman*, *Muhammad – A Western Attempt to Understand Islam*, *Christianity and Islam* and *Islam: A Short History*.

RONAN BENNETT

Ronan Bennett, whose works include three novels, several screenplays for film and television and a memoir, spent two years of his young adult life in prison as a result of the Troubles in Ireland. Exonerated, he went on to earn a PhD in history at London University. His most recent novel, *The Catastrophist*, was short-listed for the Whitbread novel award. He is a regular contributor to the *Observer*, the *Guardian*, *The London Review of Books* and other publications.

MARTIN BELL

Martin Bell was born in Suffolk in 1938 and served in its Regiment. He worked as a reporter for BBC News from 1962 to 1997 and was assigned to eighty countries and eleven wars, beginning in Vietnam and ending in Bosnia, where he was wounded. In 1997 he left the BBC to stand as an Independent candidate in the Tatton constituency in the General Election; he won by more than 11,000 votes, and so became the only Independent MP in the House of Commons. Bell served on the Standards and Privileges Committee, and was active in a number of causes, including the campaign to win compensation for the former prisoners of war of the Japanese. In 2001, Bell was appointed by UNICEF UK as Special Representative for Humanitarian Intervention. In that capacity, in October 2001, he visited UNICEF projects and Afghan refugees on the border between Afghanistan and Tadjikistan.

CHRIS BELLAMY, PhD

Chris Bellamy is Professor of Military Science at Cranfield University and heads its MSc program in Global Security. Bellamy began his career as a professional soldier, but had to leave the Army on medical grounds. He then pursued a career as an academic and journalist, during which time he found himself in real conflicts. From 1990 to 1997 he was Defence Correspondent for the *Independent* and reported from the Gulf War in 1990–91, from Bosnia from 1992–96, and from Chechnya in 1995.

DAVID BELLAMY, OBE, BSc, PhD, HON FLS

David Bellamy is a lecturer in Botany at the University of Durham, a special professor of Botany at the University of Nottingham and a visiting professor at Massey University. Bellamy is also the director of Botanical Enterprises Ltd, the founder of the National Heritage Conservatory Foundation and the Conservation Foundation. Also a member of various professional committees, Bellamy is the winner of the UNEP Global 500. His television credits include *Life in Our Sea*, *Bellamy on Botany*, *A Welsh Herbal*, and *Paradise Ploughed*. Bellamy is the author of several books including *The World of Plants*, *Il Libro Verde*, *The Queen's Hidden Garden* and *Tomorrow's Earth*.

RACHEL BILLINGTON

Rachel Billington is the author of fifteen novels, two works of non-fiction and eight childrens' books. She is Vice-President of English PEN and co-editor of the national newspaper for prisoners, *InsideTime*. Her new novel, *A Woman's Life*, will be published in February 2002.

CARYL CHURCHILL

Since the mid-70s, Caryl Churchill has ranked among the best-known political playwrights in England. Her work deals with a variety of issues, yet she reaches audiences from across the political spectrum. Her plays include *Owners*, *Traps*, *Shining in Buckinghamshire*,

Vinegar Tom, *Cloud Nine*, *Top Girls*, *Serious Money*, *Mad Forest*, *The Skriker*, *Blue Heart* and *Far Away*.

SIR TERENCE CONRAN

Terence Conran is one of the world's best-known designers, restaurateurs and retailers. He founded the Habitat chain of stores that brought good, modern design within reach of the general population and established the retail group Storehouse, which includes Heal's among others. In the 90s, Conran built another impressive group of companies, Conran Holdings, involved in design, retailing and restaurants. He owns Conran shops and restaurants around the world and his design projects have included Ocean Terminal in Edinburgh, Rex Bar in Iceland, and the Great Eastern Hotel in London. Terence Conran's books include *The Essential House Book*, *Terence Conran on Design*, *The Essential Garden Book*, *Q&A: A Sort of Autobiography* and *Alcazar to Zinc: the story of Conran Restaurants*.

WILLIAM DALRYMPLE

William Dalrymple was born in Scotland and brought up on the shores of the Firth of Forth. He has written a number of highly acclaimed, award-winning books on travel, including *In Xanadu*, *City of Djinns*, *From the Holy Mountain* and *The Age of Kali: Indian Travels & Encounters*. Dalrymple's writing has appeared in national magazines and newspapers such as the *New Statesman* and the *Independent* and he was recently elected the youngest Fellow of the Royal Society of Literature and the Royal Asiatic Society.

JASON ELLIOT

Jason Elliot is the author of the award-winning book on Afghanistan, *An Unexpected Light*, and is currently working on his next book about Iran. Elliot has travelled extensively in countries of the Islamic world over the past fifteen years.

PAUL FOOT

Author, journalist and reporter Paul Foot writes a column for the *Daily Mirror* and *Private Eye*. Foot is the recipient of numerous awards, including Journalist of the Year, the Orwell Prize for Journalism, and Campaigning Journalist of the Decade. He has written many books, including, *Immigration and Race in British Politics*, *Red Shelley*, *The Helen Smith Story*, *Murder at the Farm: Who Killed Carl Bridgewater?* and *Articles of Resistance*.

STEPHEN JAY GOULD, PhD

Stephen Jay Gould is Professor of Geology at Harvard University and is also curator for Invertebrate Paleontology at Harvard's Museum of Comparative Zoology. The author of 300 consecutive essays for his monthly column 'This View of Life' in *Natural History* magazine, Gould has also penned over 20 bestselling books, and has written nearly a thousand scientific papers. In addition, he has received numerous awards, including the MacArthur Foundation Prize Fellowship, the prestigious Medal of Edinburgh, and the Silver National Medal of the Zoology Society of London.

ASSAD HAFEEZ, MD

Dr Assad Hafeez is a paediatrician living in Islamabad. He works with the charity Child Advocacy International providing medical aid to women and children in the Afghan refugee camps on the border between Afghanistan and Pakistan. He contributes regular diary entries to the online publication *Out There News*.

SUHEIR HAMMAD

Suheir Hammad, Palestinian–American poet and political activist, has published a book of poems, *Born Palestinian, Born Black*, a memoir, *Drops of this Story* and is prominently featured in *Listen Up! An Anthology of Spoken Word Poetry*. Hammad is the recipient of the Audre Lourde Writing Award, the Morris Center for Healing Poetry Award and a New York Mills Artist Residency in Minnesota, US. Hammad has read her work on BBC radio, and on stage at the Globe.

KATHARINE HAMNETT

Katharine Hamnett studied fashion at art school in London, then worked as a freelance designer, setting up her own business, Katharine Hamnett Designs, in 1979. She draws inspiration for designs from work-wear and also from social movements, such as the peace movement, which she actively supports. Hamnett's inspiration is evident through her creation of 'logo' T-shirts that advertise social and political messages. Her tops have sported messages including, 'Save the Rainforest', 'Cancel the Third World Debt', 'Life is Sacred', 'Global Aid to Afghanistan Now', and 'Save Democracy'. Hamnett is the winner of the Fashion Designer of the Year award (1984) and the British Clothing and Knitting Council Expert Award. She is currently a professor of Fashion and Textiles at the London Institute.

THE RIGHT REVEREND RICHARD HARRIES, BISHOP OF OXFORD

Before becoming the Bishop of Oxford in 1987, The Right Reverend Richard Harries was the Dean of King's College, a parish priest and lecturer in Christian Doctrine and Ethics. He is a fellow of King's College and an Honorary Doctor of Divinity at the University of London. Harries has written 18 books including *Art and the Beauty of God*, in addition to his numerous contributions to several national newspapers and journals. He is the chairman of the Church of England Board for Social Responsibility, The House of Bishop's Working Party on Issues in Human Sexuality and the Council of Christians and Jews. Harries is also a board member of Christian Aid, the International Interfaith Foundation and a founding member of the Abrahamic Group.

ROBERT JENSEN, PhD

Robert Jensen is an associate professor in the School of Journalism at the University of Texas. He is author of *Writing Dissent: Taking Radical Ideas from the Margins to the Mainstream* and co-author with Gail Dines and Ann Russo of *Pornography: The Production and Consumption of Inequality*. He is a member of the Nowar Collective, and is a regular contributor to newspapers in the United States on foreign policy, politics and race.

TERRY JONES

Writer, film director and performer Terry Jones is best known for his television and film work with *Monty Python*. He directed *Monty Python and the Holy Grail*, *Life of Brian*, *Meaning of Life*, *Personal Services*, *Erik the Viking* and *The Wind in the Willows*. Television credits include *Crusades*, *Ancient Inventions* and *Hidden Histories*. Jones is the author of *Chaucer's Knight*, *Fairy Tales*, *Fantastic Stories*, *Nicobobinus*, *The Curse of the Vampire's Socks*, *The Knight and the Squire*, *The Lady and the Squire*, *Attacks of Opinion*, and *Who Murdered Chaucer?*

DOMINIQUE LAPIERRE

Dominique Lapierre is a former *Paris-Match* correspondent and the author of numerous international bestselling books including *Is Paris Burning?*, *City of Joy*, *Freedom at Midnight*, *O, Jerusalem*, *Beyond Love* and *Five Past Midnight in Bhopal*, several of which have been made into films. A humanitarian and phil-anthropist, Lapierre donates half his royalties to support humanitarian causes in India.

ANNIE LENNOX

Born and raised in Scotland, Annie Lennox briefly attended London's Royal Academy of Music before joining the band The Tourists in the late 1970s. Best known for her band the Eurythmics, formed with Dave Stewart in 1980, Annie Lennox helped create one of the most popular sounds of the 80s. In 1990, Lennox released her first solo album *Diva*, which sold over two million copies in the United States alone, and was nominated for three Grammy awards. Annie Lennox has also been actively involved in several charity and volunteer organizations, including Greenpeace and Amnesty International.

RAHUL MAHAJAN

Rahul Mahajan is a doctoral candidate in physics at the University of Texas at Austin and serves on the National Board of Peace Action, the largest grass-roots peace organization in the United States and is a member of the Nowar Collective. Mahajan has written for *Newsday*, *Houston Chronicle*, *The Hindu* in India, *Middle East Times* in Egypt, and others. He is the author of the soon to be published *The New Crusade: America's War on Terrorism*.

PAUL MARSDEN, MP

Before his career as a Labour MP for Shrewsbury and Atcham, Paul Marsden worked as a Quality Assurance Manager at Taylor Woodrow Construction, was employed at NatWest Bank, and Mitel Telecoms. As an MP, Marsden has presented bills on Cancer Care, Health Care Standards for the Elderly and Recycling. In 2000, Marsden spoke out on BBC *Panorama* against the government over the fuel crisis and has publicly opposed GM crops and tuition fees. Paul is Vice-Chair of Labour Against the War.

JAMES MAWDSLEY

James Mawdsley was brought up in Lancashire. He went to Bristol University to study physics and philosophy, leaving early to live in Australia. From there he became increasingly involved in the Burmese democracy movement and was subsequently imprisoned by the Burmese government. He is author of *The Heart Must Break*, an account of what he has seen in Burma's border areas and prisons.

ADRIAN MITCHELL, FRSL

Poet and playwright Adrian Mitchell served in the Royal Air Force before becoming a reporter for the *Oxford Mail* and the *Evening Standard*. Mitchell received the Granada fellowship in the Arts at University of Lancaster and a fellowship at the Center for the Humanities at Wesleyan University, USA, and has been awarded an Honorary Doctorate at North London University. Mitchell has been the resident writer at Sherman Theatre and Unicorn Theatre. His plays include *Tyger*, *Man Friday*, *Mind Your Head*, *The White Deer* and *Anna on Anna*. Mitchell has also written for opera and film and is the author of several novels, books of poetry and children's books.

GEORGE MONBIOT, CBE

George Monbiot is an environmental and human rights campaigner and writer. After working on land tenure issues in Asia, Africa and Latin America, he founded a land rights movement in Britain called *The Land is Ours*. Monbiot makes regular radio and TV appearances and writes for the *Guardian* newspaper and is the author of *Captive State*.

COURTTIA NEWLAND

Courttia Newland is the author of titles including *The Scholar* and *Society Within Afrobeat*. Selected by the British Council to represent the new wave of British writing, Newland toured in the Czech Republic with Hanif Kureishi in 1999. He is the co-editor of *IC3: The Penguin Book of New Black Writing in Britain*. Newland has recently cut his teeth in the world of theatre with his company, The Post Office Theatre, Co. His latest novel, *Snakeskin*, is published in Spring 2002.

BEN OKRI, FRSL

Author and poet Ben Okri pursued a career as a presenter and broadcaster at the BBC before becoming a full-time writer. A member of the Society of Authors, PEN International and the recipient of an Honorary Doctorate of literature at the University of Westminster, Okri is the winner of many prizes including the Commonwealth Prize for Africa, the Paris Review Prize for Fiction, the Booker Prize, Premio Grinane Cavour and Premio Palmi. Okri has written several books, including *Flowers and Shadows*, *Incidents at the Shrine*, *An African Elegy*, *Astonishing the Gods*, *Dangerous Love*, *Infinite Riches*, *The Famished Road* and *Mental Fight*.

JOSEPH OLSHAN

Joseph Olshan is the award-winning author of seven novels, including *Clara's Heart*, *Nightswimmer*, and most recently, *In Clara's Hands*. Olshan has also written non-fiction articles and essays for many publications, including the *New York Times Magazine* and the *Washington Post*. Additionally, Olshan is the editorial director of Delphinium Books and lives in New York City.

MATTHEW PARRIS

Matthew Parris is a freelance broadcaster and columnist for *The Times*. Parris is also the recipient of several awards and is the author of books on politics, humour and travel, including *The Great Unfrocked*, *Read My Lips*, *Off Message* and *The Outsider*.

JONATHON PORRITT

Jonathon Porritt is Co-founder and Programme Director of Forum for the Future. He is a leading writer, broadcaster and commentator on sustainable development, and his most recent book is *Playing Safe: Science and the Environment*. In October 2000 he was appointed by the Prime Minister as Chairman of the new UK Sustainable Development Commission. He is also a member of the Board of the South West Regional Development Agency, and is Co-Director of The Prince of Wales's Business and Environment Programme.

GEOFFREY ROBERTSON QC

Geoffrey Robertson is the author of *Crimes Against Humanity: The Struggle for Global Justice*. He is Head of Doughty Street Chambers, a Recorder and Visiting Professor in Human Rights law at Birkbeck College. He has argued many landmark human rights cases in the courts of England and the Commonwealth and in the European Court of Human Rights, and has led missions for Amnesty and Human Rights Watch. He is the author of several legal textbooks, including *Freedom, the Individual and the Law* and *Media Law*, and of a memoir, *The Justice Game*.

ANITA RODDICK, OBE

Anita Roddick opened a small shop in a back street of Brighton selling beauty products made from natural products, not tested on animals, and supplied in refillable containers in 1976. In the Body Shop she created a company with attitude that is known around the world for both its products and its principles. Her dedication to ecology and the Third World has resulted in her book *Take It Personally*, which explores the myths of globalization.

EDWARD W. SAID, PhD

Edward W. Said is a Professor of English and Comparative Literature at Columbia University and has lectured at more than 150 colleges and universities worldwide. He is a regular contributor to the *Guardian*, *Le Monde Diplomatique* and the Arab-language daily *al-Hayat*, printed in every Arab capital in the world. His writing, translated into 14 languages, includes 10 books, among them, *Orientalism*, *The World, the Text and the Critic*, *Blaming the Victims*, *Culture and Imperialism* and *Peace and Its Discontents: Essays on Palestine in the Middle East Peace Process*.

ZIAUDDIN SARDAR, PhD

Ziauddin Sardar is a writer and cultural critic. He has published over 35 books on various aspects of Islam, the Middle East, science policy, culture studies and related subjects including *Postmodernism and the Other*, *Orientalism*, *The Consumption of Kuala Lumpur*, *Introducing Islam*, *The Future of Muslim Civilisation* and *Islamic Futures: The Shape of Ideas to Come*. Sardar is a regular contributor to the *New Statesman* and the *Observer*, and is a Visiting Professor of Postcolonial Studies at City University.

AHDAF SOUEIF

Ahdaf Soueif was born in Cairo and spent part of her childhood in London. She is the author of *Aisha*, *Sandpiper*, *The Map of Love* and *In the Eye of the Sun*, among others.

MARK STEEL

Mark Steel has performed as a stand-up comedian since 1983. He co-wrote and performed four series of *The Mark Steel Solution* and has written and performed three series of *The Mark Steel Lecture* for Radio 4. He has hosted the Radio 5 sports program *Extra Time* and written two books *It's Not a Runner Bean* and *Reasons to Be Cheerful*. Mark Steel writes for the *Guardian,* the *Independent* and the *New Statesman*.

TERRY WAITE, CBE

Terry Waite, envoy of the Archbishop of Canterbury, international humanitarian, and former Beirut hostage is committed to responsible leadership for social justice. As the Archbishop's special envoy, he was particularly involved in negotiations to secure the release of hostages held in the Middle East; between 1982 and the end of 1986, fourteen hostages, for whom he was interceding, were released. Terry Waite was kidnapped in Beirut in January 1987 while involved in secret negotiations to win the release of hostages held in Lebanon. He was not released until November 1991. He is the author of two volumes of memoirs, *Taken on Trust* and *Travels with a Primate*.

NATASHA WALTER

Natasha Walter is the author of *The New Feminism* and editor of *On the Move: Feminism for a New Generation*. She writes a column for the *Independent*.

MARTIN WRIGHT

Martin Wright is Editor of *Green Futures*. Martin has written and broadcast widely on environmental issues in the UK and overseas, has contributed articles and photos to a range of publications, including the *Observer*, *The Times*, the *Guardian*, the *Independant On Sunday*, *Newsweek* and *New Scientist* and won the Environment Council's Science and Environment Journalist of the Year Award. He has written and produced documentaries on these issues for UK independent television, and broadcast on BBC and independent radio, and on the BBC world service.

Editor's Biography

Anna Kiernan is a freelance writer and editor and has reviewed for *The Times Literary Supplement*, *The Big Issue* and *Stealth*, amongst others. She is also a part-time lecturer in Media and Culture at Essex University. Her MA thesis was entitled, 'What does multicultural-ism mean for the white literary imagination?'. She is currently working on her first novel.

The appalling events in America were a terrible reminder, if any were needed, of the unstable and violent world we live in. War Child condemns those atrocities, as we do all acts of violence against innocent people the world over.

Conflict is born out of the hatred of adults, but it is invariably children who suffer most. Be it those killed, maimed or orphaned in America, or the millions who continue to suffer in Afghanistan and throughout the world, if we adults do not take an active responsibility for children's well being, the future will offer no more hope than the present.

This should be a time for reflection, not only on our own vulnerability, but also on the precarious existence of the millions of our fellow human beings whose suffering shows no sign of abating.

War Child will continue to work towards a more peaceful world. We will intervene in emergency situations wherever appropriate and effective. In the longer term we continue to focus on education and communications, in the firm belief that ignorance is the life blood of conflict.

War Child is currently working in Central Asia to provide emergency assistance to the people of Afghanistan, and continues to provide long term aid to children and their families in Africa and the Balkans.

War Child
PO Box 20231
London NW5 3WP
Tel. 020 7916 9276
Fax. 020 7916 9280
info@warchild.globalnet.co.uk
www.warchild.org.uk